FINAL CURTAINS

NED SHERRIN

D0130143

First published in 2008
by Oldie Publications Ltd
65 Newman Street, London W1T 3EG
www.theoldie.co.uk

Copyright © Oldie Publications, 2008
Foreword © Victoria Mather, 2008

ISBN-10: 1901170071
ISBN-13: 978-1901170078

A catalogue record for this book
is available from the British Library

Typeset in 10/13pt Garamond Premier Pro
Printed by CPI Cox & Wyman

FINAL CURTAINS
TOP-DRAWER MEMORIAL SERVICES
1993-2007

Contents

Foreword

AFTER A PARTICULARLY grim day at the Royal Brompton Hospital Ned felt in need of a vodka martini, as one does, and he always did at 6pm. I popped back to his flat to get the wherewithal: vodka, a whisper of martini, lemon and a silver cocktail shaker. Ice I begged from Matron. I shook and stirred according to Ned's croaked instructions and held the result to his lips in a paper cup. There was a sip, then a beady eye, then a furious croak: 'Too much lemon.'

Standards. Ned Sherrin had immutable standards, most particularly about production. He was as excited, and as critical, about a first night as about the last act in the lives of the celebrated and the maverick. He was, as Keith Waterhouse and I recommended to Richard Ingrams, the perfect person to be Britain's first and only memorial service reviewer. Being, if anything, rather keener on the last acts than the first nights as the after-party happened at lunch time.

There's a severe ticking-off in this anthology of columns he wrote for *The Oldie* on the regrettable modern shift to memorial services at 3pm: not enough time for a good lunch, the risky prospect of tea afterwards rather than proper drinks, and possible interference with the Sherrin routine of the 6pm martini followed by *The Archers*. Anyone slipping into the next room with Canon Henry Scott Holland receives a veiled reprimand for lack of originality.

I first knew Ned Sherrin some 30 years ago. Like my father, he was a theatre director. Unlike anyone else he was also a wit, raconteur, broadcaster, writer, producer, author and polymath. I met Ned and his Gladstone bag (a present from Caryl Brahms) on the first night of *The Sloane Ranger Review*, to which I had contributed in some of the original articles published in *Harpers & Queen*, and was terrified. I later became his head girl on *Loose Ends*, to be joined by Emma Freud and Carol Thatcher, and was happy. We both loved oysters, lobster, grouse, potted shrimps, *The Archers* and the Bunn family at Hickstead. I wouldn't give in on tripe (a Ned speciality, simmered in milk), he would not countenance rice in any form. When Ned was at the

Royal Marsden I was honoured to be referred to as his daughter, his wife and his mother... mildly irked on this one ...and finally, when I arrived with fish pie and chilled white wine for supper, to see the Sherrin shoulders, thin and frail now, shaking with laughter: 'New Matron thinks you're my mistress'.

I remember the Ned who made the fatherly speech at my wedding; the Ned for whom I gave birthday parties: he arrived at his 60th on the back of Andy Kershaw's motor bike and left Frankie Howerd behind on our sofa for what seemed like several days. The Ned who loved A N Wilson's slow-roasted lamb (as recommended by his favourite cook, Jennifer Paterson), with 20 cloves of garlic that I cooked for his 75th birthday. He was such a foodie that it was a close run thing what presents he enjoyed most during his illness: the caviar delivery wars between Dame Judi Dench and the Broadway legend Marti Stevens, or a Get Well card signed by the entire cast of *The Archers*. Oysters were the last thing he ate, brought round by Simon Parker-Bowles from Green's.

Most of all, Ned Sherrin loved, and collected, anecdote and gossip. Memorial services are anecdote central, gleaned from the addresses and tributes, as this anthology reveals. Whether the famous: as in Ronnie Corbett on Ronnie Barker (page 156) – 'Ronnie would write a sketch; I would queue for his lunch'; or the famous-to-those-on-the-inside-track: David Land (page 20), who did such a wonderful job managing the Theatre Royal, Brighton, created a company called Hope & Glory so that he could answer the telephone 'Land, of Hope & Glory'.

I particularly like the story from Charles Wintour's memorial (page 44), during which it was remembered that the young Tom Stoppard had applied for a job to the great editor of the *Evening Standard*, expressing an interest in politics. 'So, Mr Stoppard, what is the name of the Home Secretary?' Small Pause. 'Mr Wintour, I said I was interested in politics. I did not say I was obsessed.' I particularly recommend the Bernard Levin reading on Shakespeare (page 128), an instruction, even benediction, to us all.

There's real brio in this anthology. Ned was not frightened of death. He believed it was a gate to go through. A loving and understanding God would be on the other side. Preferably you should go through the gates to the sound of trumpets and the choir of St Bride's. I hope I didn't let him down at the end. At the funeral the Gladstone bag was on his coffin together with 25 kilos of John Carter's red-rich flowers that one could have taken on tour. He left precious few clues for his memorial, other than to say he wanted Maria Friedman to sing *Not Funny*, which Ned wrote with Gerard Kenny, who accompanied her, and for Clarke Peters to sing *Talking to My Pal* from *Pal Joey*. For the rest, he asked 'To be surprised'. I hope he would have been, at least by the Bullshot Bar manned by Neil and Christine Hamilton, Carol Thatcher and Viscountess Gormanston on entry to the Actors' Church. A bullshot was a favourite Ned drink. Many Ned fans asked for theirs with milk and sugar.

I don't think he'd have been surprised that Judi Dench flew back from Panama, where she was filming Bond, to read two lines of poetry in farewell, or that Tom Conti reinterpreted lines from *Jeffrey Bernard is Unwell* just for him, or that Victor Spinetti reduced the church to tears with The Rev Eli Jenkins's *Sunset Poem* from *Under Milk Wood*. Or that his godson, Charlie Bunn, read so beautifully from *The Great Gatsby*. He would love it if this book isn't just the fun of the anecdotes and gossip but also a help towards original readings and comforting traditional psalms and hymns for us all. He never meant it to be a book, so that's a surprise. I think he would be thrilled.

Victoria Mather, London, 2008

Sam Wanamaker

1919-1993

Southwark Cathedral

THE LIFE OF SAM Wanamaker was celebrated on a sparkling spring morning a few hundred yards from the budding Globe Theatre which he had spent the last 40 years of his life creating. Those who chose to walk to Southwark Cathedral round the Clink, where once only a dirty brass plate on a brewery wall marked the site of Shakespeare's playhouse, could already witness the first shoots of his ambitious recreation. Great wooden structures hedge a pit which awaits its groundlings as the pioneer towers await their neighbours.

The cathedral itself, where a tablet to Sam will soon sit beside Shakespeare's own, was full and overflowing. Sam's acting and his directing were both as muscular as his fundraising, and he could not have found a more vigorous opening chorus than *He Who Would Valiant Be*.

Keith Baxter's prologue to the play was an eloquent testimony to Sam's career since World War Two – not forgetting that it was Wanamaker and not John Wayne who actually landed on some Pacific Island – was it Iwo Jima? Baxter's striking metaphor took the Globe as Sam's search for his Grail – glimpsed before he died.

Mark Rylance spoke Maxwell Anderson's lines to celebrate Sam's Broadway debut in *Joan of Lorraine*, and Rosemary Harris spoke Shaw's St Joan's refusal to recant.

Warren Mitchell, speaking as 'a non-practising Jewish atheist – thank God!', relished Sam's lone amusement when, from the same pulpit on the Bard's birthday, he had Alf Garnetted Shakespeare to an uncomprehending congregation. Mitchell was billed to speak about Sam's production of *The Threepenny Opera*, ahead of its time in the '50s. He told of Sam's endless reassurance to the disenchanted cast previewing in Brighton with the constant reiteration, 'Trust me, theatrically it works' – as will the Globe.

Edward Downes celebrated Sam's passion for opera. Leo McKern read Genesis. Noah's construction of the Ark recalled Sam's edifice on the South Bank. His bottomless international begging bowl was epitomised by Norbert Kentrup revelling in Falstaff's honour speech in German.

Michael Perry remembered Sam's Christmas card, posted days before he died: 'Sorry I won't be with you to share the celebrations, but I have been celebrating anyway.'

Before the stirring *Battle Hymn Of The Republic* – his eyes had seen the Glory – Diana Rigg, with a passion only Sybil Thorndike might have exceeded, called for a 'Muse of Fire', envisaging the day when the Globe's cock-pit will 'hold the vastie fields of France' and contain within its 'Wooden O, the very Caskes that did affright the Ayre at Agincourt.'

***He Who Would Valiant Be** (John Bunyan)*
He who would valiant be 'gainst all disaster,
Let him in constancy follow the Master.
There's no discouragement shall make him once relent,
His first avowed intent to be a pilgrim.

Who so beset him round with dismal stories
Do but themselves confound – his strength the more is.
No foes shall stay his might; though he with giants fight:
He will make good his right to be a pilgrim.

Brian Johnston,
CBE, MC
1912-1994
Westminster Abbey

AN ABBEY MEMORIAL SERVICE which starts with *The Eton Boating Song*, and plays you out with *Underneath the Arches*, starts and finishes strongly. The Abbey stage managers never let down those it celebrates. You can rely on heart-stopping moments which upstage the rhetoric, the singing and the setting – but never the subject. Sybil Thorndike had her trumpets – she was mad for trumpets – to blow her away to the other side. With Laurence Olivier it was the parade of great actors bearing his emblems and awards. For Kenneth Macmillan it was a child fluting the *Pie Jesu* from aloft.

For 'Johnners' it was the Grenadiers. Two young Guards musicians playing the *Grenadiers' Return* slow-marched the length of the nave, the quire and the sacrarium, drumming and piping the tune in honour of a Guards MC. The drummer cannot have been born when Brian turned 60.

Brother Christopher read Psalm 15 – 'Lord, who shall dwell in Thy tabernacle?' Son, Barry, read his godfather William Douglas Hume's *A Glorious Game, Say We*: 'Yes, cricket will live till the trumpet trumps/ From the wide, pavillioned sky/And time, the umpire lays low the stumps/ As his scythe goes sweeping by...'

Colin Cowdrey and John Major gave addresses from parallel pulpits. Cowdrey represented the cricketing profession with the eloquence and humour of those memorable amateurs. The Prime Minister well conveyed the affection in which the ordinary man held Johnners.

After Michael Denison had done justice to Cardus on the outbreak of war seen from the Long Room, Richard Stilgoe, our leading occasional versifier alluded to 'the bowler's holding...' without offending Dean, Chapter or Archbishop Runcie, and trumpeted two corking couplets. Of Brian's arrival in Heaven: 'He talks to total strangers,/Calls the Angel Gabriel "Angers"';

and of his new role as a heavenly greeter: 'When St Peter's done the honours,/He will pass you on to Johnners.' You will recognise the seraph by his 'ears like wings and correspondent shoes' and the proffered 'angel-cake'. The Prime Minister had not been perfectly briefed. The moving poem *From a Blind Listener* was not, as he heralded it, 'by a little boy' (charming image) but by the mature Melvin Collins who read it strongly: 'He was a friend to those who never knew him,/Eyes to those who cannot see...'

Eton Boating Song *(William Johnson Cory)*
Jolly boating weather,
And a hay harvest breeze,
Blade on the feather,
Shade off the trees,
Swing swing together,
With your bodies between your knees,
Swing swing together,
With your bodies between your knees.

Rugby may be more clever,
Harrow may make more row,
But we'll row for ever,
Steady from stroke to bow,
And nothing in life shall sever,
The chain that is round us now,
And nothing in life shall sever,
The chain that is round us now.

Mervyn Stockwood

1913-1995

Cathedral of St Saviour & St Mary Overie, Southwark

I VERY NEARLY MISSED THIS send-off because of the newly fashionable time of three o'clock. I rather prefer the good old noon-and-on-to-lunch-and-reminiscence.

Bishop Mervyn's memorial was distinguished by a remarkable sermon by Lord Runcie. There had been scant warning of the occasion and I only knew about it because Robert Runcie had asked me if I knew any Mervyn jokes. Sadly, none he could use. I'd arrived without ticket and was cast into the outer darkness by a grim woman in a black headband who said sternly, 'You'll have to sit in the black seats.' I found a marginally more convenient spot among some anoraked priests on grey seats at the back.

The service was beautifully sung and spoken; but its feature was Archbishop Runcie's wonderfully warm evocation of Mervyn, taking his text from *Ecclesiastes* ('Cast thy bread upon the waters...') which he defined as 'the most mysterious and cynical book in the Bible'. He summoned up Mervyn's generosity, his conviviality, his politics and his spirituality in a variety of well-crafted phrases – his own and the scriptures': 'The heart of a wise man inclines to the right, the heart of a fool to the left...'

Quoting Mervyn arriving at the University Church, 'Show me where to kiss the Remnants or are they already sitting in their pews?' His boredom with 'working parties' – 'paralysis by analysis.' 'A socialist who also loved the upper reaches of the social scale.'

He mocked the traditional valued judgment after death – 'He was all of a piece.' Mervyn, he insisted, was a generous mixture of men – 'Is it a bad thing to be more than one man?'

Finally, he could not resist the ultimate Stockwood anecdote. At the last Lambeth conference, Mervyn was on the list of Bishops outed by Tatchell's 'thought police'. The Bishop of Bath and Wells rang to warn him. Mervyn cut him short. 'Jim,' he said, 'I couldn't care tuppence. And if the press get on to you, tell them I've had a lot of women too!'

Ecclesiastes 11:1-4
Cast thy bread upon the waters:
for thou shalt find it after many days.
Give a portion to seven, and also to eight;
for thou knowest not what evil shall be upon the earth.
If the clouds be full of rain,
they empty themselves upon the earth:
and if the tree fall toward the south, or toward the north,
in the place where the tree falleth, there it shall be.
He that observeth the wind shall not sow;
and he that regardeth the clouds shall not reap.

John Osborne

1929-1994

St Giles-in-the-Fields

THE OLD INNOVATOR KEPT it up even beyond the grave. Few of the theatrical Great and Good who filled St Giles on a fine Friday morning 'to celebrate the life and work of John Osborne' had entered that church before.

The word was that Helen Osborne got a special deal for the beautiful 260-year-old Flitcroft interior. Bigger than St Paul's, Covent Garden, friendlier than St Martin's, more modest than St James', St Giles perfectly hosted a service nicely judged to reflect John's obsessions and achievements, right down to the notorious notice on the door forbidding entry to certain persons, so ludicrously objected to by Ms Purves.

There was Grey Gowrie to read from 1 Corinthians, 15: 'For the trumpet shall sound, and the dead shall be raised incorruptible.' There was Maggie Smith and more trumpets – this time Bunyan's: 'So he passed over and the trumpets sounded for him on the other side.' (We also had them at Sybil Thorndike's do; but let that pass.)

Richard Griffiths read the *Henry IV* epilogue: 'I was lately here in the end of a displeasing play, to pray your patience for it and to promise you a better.' Dirk Bogarde contributed Jeremy Taylor's *The Rule and Exercises of Holy Dying*. Yvonne Kenny and Robert Johnston sang Purcell (*Fairest Isle*) and Britten (*St Nicholas*). Elgar (*Enigma*) and Vaughan Williams (*The Lark Ascending*) were separated by an American, Nat D Ayer. Michael Ball sang his infectious *If You Were the Only Girl in the World*.

Excerpts from Osborne's *Look Back In Anger* and *Déjà Vu,* read by Peter Egan, were divided by a recording of Olivier singing *Why Should I Care?* Edward Fox, in Housman's words, evoked John's lost Shropshire neighbours, 'Clunton and Clunbury, Clungunford and Clun... the quietest places under the sun.' David Hare's address was authoritative, affectionate and funny, he too picked up on Osborne's Shropshire connection: 'I lift up my eyes to the blue, remembered hills, and they call back "Shove off!" He placed him accurately as English theatre's 'vital voice... he knocked down the door and a whole generation piled through.' He emphasised his gift for friendship – 'One of the best prospects of gossip and entertainment'; the storms he could cause in a theatre; and his zest for living: 'I never had lunch in Brighton without wanting to take a woman to bed.' Nor did he ignore the acting career – 'Playing Hamlet on Hayling Island like a leering milk roundsman' – or the fraught relationship with Nellie Beatrice: 'Well, he certainly put a lot into it.' And we certainly got a lot out of it!

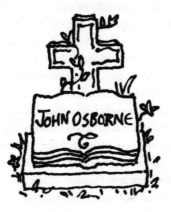

Epilogue, Henry IV, Part 2 *(William Shakespeare)*
First my fear; then, my curtsy; last my speech. My fear is your displeasure: my curtsy, my duty: and my speech, to beg your pardon. If you look for a good speech now, you undo me; for what I have to say is of mine own making; and what indeed I should say will, I doubt, prove mine own marring. But to the purpose, and so to the venture...

...I was lately here in the end of a displeasing play, to pray your patience for it and to promise you a better. I did mean indeed to pay you with this; which, if like an ill venture it come unluckily home, I break, and you, my gentle creditors, lose.

R E S Wyatt

1901-1995

St John's Wood Church

'WHAT ARE YOU DOING here, if I might so enquire?' asked J J Warr politely as we walked away from R E S Wyatt's memorial service in St John's Wood Church, a deep slip-catch away from Lords, to which J J was going on for a drink with a lot of other initials. *Oldie* readers should be able to supply the surnames if I reel off D C S, M K J, F G, D R W, G H G, Sir M C, E W, D L, T G, Mrs P B H, and A C D (Ingleby-Mackenzie, the last, was the nearest thing to a boy cricketer in the church).

The setting was perfect, a deep cherry-red Madonna and two huge vases of summer flowers the only focus of colour against the unrelieved cricket cream of the walls. Well, I was there because, unlike Tim Rice, I saw Wyatt play and because I did (for Radio 4) the last interview with him, when he and Mollie, now his widow, entertained me in Cornwall. His nut-brown pate and twinkling eyes remained a vivid memory as memorialists filleted a past of courageous hundreds, broken limbs, smacked jaws, inspiring leadership, egalitarian example and gentlemanly forgiveness.

'The truth is,' wrote R C Robertson-Glasgow of Wyatt (so glad that on second thoughts Warwickshire named his stand the 'R E S' not the 'Bob'), 'he is part artist, part workman... I don't know if he is a great batsman: but he is a great cricketer, a great cricketer of yesterday and today in performance and of many tomorrows in the chronicles of fame.'

It fell to his young cousin, Woodrow, who idolised him as a child, and to Tim Rice, his Cornish neighbour, to chronicle a life which stretched from Grace to Gough. They did it with warmth. His son, Jonathan, whose scalp will brown up as nicely as his father's given another good summer, read Moult's *Close of Play*: 'How shall we live, now that the summer's ended/ And bat at ball (too soon!) are put aside...?'

The choir sang Mozart, *Laudate Dominum*, and Brahms, *How lovely are thy dwellings.* The hymn tunes were good roast-beef stuff which suited the man – Old Hundredth, Crimond, St Clement. Lord Runcie said the prayers.

I wonder if Mr Major performed the same service for D C S that he discharged after Brian Johnston's send off? 'Can I get you a drink Denis?' Compton was famously asked at the reception, and famously replied, 'No thanks, the Prime Minister's getting me one.'

Paul Eddington, CBE

1927-1995

St Paul's Church, Covent Garden

David Land

1918-1995

Theatre Royal, Brighton

STAR AND SHOWMAN. FEW faces had more public currency than Paul Eddington's, few less than David Land's. Within six days these distinguished lives were celebrated: Eddington's at St Paul's, Covent Garden; Land's at his Brighton Theatre Royal. Both boasted standing room only.

Along with Lord Runcie, Alan Bennett is our most eloquent elegiast. He was abroad, so Toby Eddington read his apology. Paul always saw Alan's plays. Alan never got to Paul's performances so, wrote Bennett, 'It is fitting that I cannot be here.' He recalled their frivolous moments, rejecting the contemptuous term 'luvvies' in favour of 'sillies': 'If politicians and editors were as silly as we are, the world would be a better place.'

Paul's devoted doctor specialist, Roy Davies, slyly confessed to advising against a trip to Australia 'without a medical advisor – January is not a terribly busy month for medical advisors.'

Patricia Eddington bravely brought alive her husband's last moments, alert to their children's daily dramas. On hearing the word 'oxygen', he opened one eye and whispered, 'Did you say "gin"?'

Penelope Keith, Richard Briers and Dorothy Tutin read beautifully. David Storey recalled a meeting Paul engineered in his dressing room between Storey's miner father and John Gielgud, resulting in 'mutual incomprehension never seen before or since'.

Paul Eddington's was a courageous and painful progress to death. David Land's was a sudden snatch at Christmas. Tim Rice was the impresario for his tribute. Land bankrolled Rice and Lloyd Webber at the beginning of their careers. As a result, he touched theatre figures in Australia, America and Japan, who testified on film.

It was always quotable. Sarah Esdaille remembered her grandfather teasingly demanding that she eulogise him as had Yitzhak Rabin's granddaughter at the murdered man's funeral. Sadly, the occasion came so soon for Sarah, but she did him justice.

Jack Tinker reminded us of David's dismissal of his Rottingdean home – 'early ugly' – and his mock dismay when told that Sarah Bernhardt had broken her leg on the stage of his theatre: 'She's not going to sue, is she?'

We had Vera Lynn, Marti Webb, a cantor and two choirs, Rice accompanied by Lloyd Webber, perhaps the loveliest male voice in musicals (Colm Wilkinson) and, to cap it all, the Dagenham Girl Pipers. All for a much-loved man who called his firm Hope and Glory so that he could answer the phone, 'Land – of Hope and Glory!' And who, on his induction as a Doctor of Literature at Sussex University, gazed at his black hat and yellow robes and protested, 'They'll think I'm a rabbi with jaundice!'

Jessica Mitford

1917-1996

Lyric Theatre

Beryl Reid

1919-1996

St Paul's Church, Covent Garden

JESSICA 'DECCA' MITFORD'S SEND-OFF at the Lyric Theatre was a cheerful and affectionate, ramshackle affair hosted by Jon 'Packer' Snow. His characteristically Mitfordian nickname was bestowed by Decca when he successfully packed a gravestone and two Chas 'n' Di musical wedding mugs for her and dispatched them to San Francisco where they arrived intact. John Mortimer covered the Hons and Rebels years. Polly Toynbee and Helena Kennedy spoke well. I wish we had included the Edna St Vincent Millay poem, 'I shall die but that is all that I shall do for Death' in *Remembrance*. James MacGibbon evoked the days when idealistic communism was part of *A Fine Old Conflict* and recalled his first meeting with Decca. In Act Two, Christopher Hitchens celebrated Decca the Muckraker. Bob Treuhaft, widower, told his favourite 'my first visit to Chatsworth' anecdote. The two children, Constancia Romilly and Benjamin Treuhaft, launched their 'Send a Pianna to Havannah' appeal, designed to get pianos into Cuba and get up the noses of the American administration. A truly Mitfordian 'tease'.

The afternoon was threaded through with film clips of Decca – particularly funny when she was viewing funeral caskets and baiting undertakers. Before ancient voices were raised in a spirited *Internationale*, Maya Angelou did a virtuoso half-hour citing Decca's determination to be introduced as her mother when they visited the unsympathetic red-neck South; and their ride through San Francisco on the backs of two 'Barnum & Bailey' circus elephants.

OPENING BERYL REID'S CELEBRATION at St Paul's, Covent Garden, Sir Harry Secombe pointed out that circus was perhaps the one bit of showbiz which Beryl had not essayed. He defined her as a real star in an age when a superstar is someone who has shaken the hand of Andrew Lloyd Webber and a megastar is someone who has declined to. Eileen Atkins was a model of eloquence, love and laughter. Their first meeting, Beryl's cats and the frankness ('I know, you were using your sincere voice') were all recalled. Your video critic [Larry Adler], on mouth-organ, accompanied Issy Van Rendwyck beautifully for Porter's *Everytime We Say Goodbye*.

Willie Rushton

1937-1996

St Paul's Church, Covent Garden

YOUR CRITIC'S RECALL OF this splendid occasion is not as authoritative as usual as he was unable to take notes. Nor could he hear everything from his choir stall. However, there was no mistaking the love and the laughter which filled the 'Actors' Church'. Canon Bill Hall processed the length of 'the most beautiful barn' to Willie's recording of the signature tune of his Australian TV show, *Our Sweet Way*. It had featured at his wedding to Dorgan when his musical director arrived to play the *Wedding March* and knew neither the tune nor the whereabouts of a score.

Editor Ingrams' reminiscences go back to Shrewsbury, where Willie arrived fully fashioned as a pocket adult and failed maths six times. When switched to biology, he contemplated the gruesome contents of a specimen bottle during an exam and, asked to describe its contents, wrote one word: 'Disgusting.'

It came as news to many that Willie's favourite instrument was the kazoo. Enough were purchased to furnish a band of nine to accompany him on the *Private Eye* recording of *Neasden*, performed with John Wells.

Wells, 'live-from-the-chancel-steps', injected some sobering intimations of mortality and still kept the laughter flowing with Willie's successful attempts to ingratiate himself with Germans in Munich ('Hello, Krautkopf!') and with the French in Paris ('Bonjour Froggy!').

All Things Bright and Beautiful was one of the two hymns Willie used to sing about the house. (The other, *Jerusalem*, closed the celebration.) The former had provided Willie with a savage ecological parody: 'All things wise and wonderful/Man will destroy them all.'

Barry Cryer daringly revealed Willie's role as Chris Evans' father, before embarking on 'Tales from the After Dinner Circuit'; particularly the pompous chairman who told Willie to be funny: 'We're paying you a lot of money, Rushton.' To which Rushton snapped: 'And most of it's for having to sit next to you.'

In 1963 Willie's lament of a Neapolitan gigolo, *Fornicazione is Italian for love*, was censored on TW3 to the chagrin, nay, tears of the singer, David Kernan. Twenty-four years on he got to sing it to universal approval. Toby Rushton read 'God Created Cricket' from his father's *Marylebone Versus the World* with a wealth of characterisation as the argument over the great summer game raged between God and the Holy Ghost: "'It shall be called Grasshopper,' smiled God, 'and we shall call the place where it is played – God's'".

Bron Waugh produced nothing as startling as his joke at Willie's funeral: 'Death is a serious business, but if Will was here today I dare say we'd be having a good laugh at the death of Sir Laurens Van der Post'; but he philosophised eloquently and amusingly on Will the soldier, eagerly embracing the rank of other rank.

He was preceded by a soaring version of *Come Sunday* by the Humphrey Lyttleton band, who, after the Blessing, processed around the church and led the congregation in a fine ramble across the Covent Garden Piazza.

Tears were inappropriate, but it was gratifying that this music brought a lump to the throat after a service which had truly reflected the wit, originality and benign genius of its subject, and the unique affection in which he was held.

Sir John Junor

1919-1997

St Bride's Church, Fleet Street

LONDON EC BECAME *BRIGADOON* for an hour in September, or at least Auchtermuchty. As we approached St Bride's, a solitary piper (Nigel Rowantree, a gamekeeper's son on a piping hot scholarship to Fettes) keened atmospherically.

Inside, the choir segued into the *The Skye Boat Song* and the rector, Canon John Oates, bidding gave us an unusually frank glimpse of the man whose life we were celebrating: 'Of unquenchable optimism, boundless energy, terrible anger and trusting sentimentality. A man who loved life, who was sharp and funny, bigoted and bloody-minded...'

The *Daily Mail* fingered those who came and those who stayed away: 'Baroness Thatcher sent Denis, but John Major turned up in person. William Hague sent his Chief of Staff...'

It took a long time to get everyone in, owing to the ebullience of one of the ushers, the genial Peter McKay, who improved thrice on the Ancient Mariner's technique, stopping one in one for a chat.

A version of *Eternal Father, Strong To Save* recalled Sir John's time with the Fleet Air Arm. 'Strong Son of Man, save those who fly/Swift-winged athwart th'unchartered sky...' The *Mail* column praised Sam Leith, a grandson, for his reading of I Corinthians, 13, 'without Tony Blair's recent hammy nuances'; a low blow from a columnist who read inaudibly extracts from Sir John's journalism. By his side, Penny Junor delivered alternate passages with exemplary warmth, clarity and wit.

Lord Rothermere, describing himself as the 'last of the old-time proprietors', praised Junor's 'humour of a particularly Scottish variety': 'He admired the Queen Mother, Marilyn Monroe and Selena Scott, Alec Douglas-Home, Victor Matthews and Bernard Ingham. The ones he loathed I shall forbear to mention, though JJ certainly did not.'

On Junor's move from *Express* to *Mail*, an *Express* editor reviled his early columns: 'Good wine clearly does not travel.' Junor replied: 'Good wine travels enormously well. Great vintages and premier crus are enjoyed all over the world; but wine from sour grapes is hardly worth bottling at all.'

We had *Ae Fond Kiss, And Then We Sever* and the devolution anthem *Flower Of Scotland*: 'Proud Edward's Army/And sent him homeward/Tae think again' – and *Auld Lang Syne*. The tear ducts were finally challenged as Nigel Rowantree piped us out to the slow air of *Highland Cathedral*.

Ae Fond Kiss, And Then We Sever *(Robert Burns)*
Ae fond kiss, and then we sever;
Ae fareweel, alas, for ever!
Deep in heart-wrung tears I'll pledge thee,
Warring sighs and groans I'll wage thee.
Who shall say that Fortune grieves him,
While the star of hope she leaves him?
Me, nae cheerful twinkle lights me;
Dark despair around benights me.

Jak (Raymond Jackson)

1927-1997

St Bride's Church, Fleet Street

ST BRIDE'S, FLEET STREET, was full of *Evening Standard* colleagues and erstwhile fellow revellers for Jak's farewell. Only Polly, his mother, who at 93 took her stall stoically, called him Raymond. Canon Oates' Bidding Prayer contained a masterpiece of understatement remembering his 'exceptional capacity for enjoying life to the full'.

General Sir Peter de la Billière was there to remind us of the fascination the Army held for Jak – especially the SAS. He was in Borneo being tattooed with a bottle of Quink ink by a Dyak head-hunter when a platoon took him under their wing. Sir Peter read from Ecclesiastes, 3: 'To every thing there is a season...'

Angus McGill read from Jak's reports as travel writer, war correspondent and roving diplomat; and Lord Rothermere delivered the popular favourite, *If I should go before the rest of you*; Joyce Grenfell's regular contribution to memorial services.

It was left to the slim, handsome, young eulogist to remember the cartoonist and his exuberant lifestyle. 'Waitah! Your finest champagne!' was his (as E J Thribb would say) catchphrase. If possible, Pol Roger, because of a family connection of that House and his French wife, Claudie. Jak's theory was 'best champagne, no hangover'. It never worked.

Many of his cartoon captions live in the memory long after the vision of his conscientious draughtsmanship has faded. One, near to home, showed two members of SOGAT standing in the bleak, empty ruins of Fleet Street. The older man waves an expansive hand: 'One day, my son, all this will be yours.' A meticulously drawn massed heap of bodies recorded the bombardment of Srebrenica above the caption 'Building a greater Serbia'. At the cash dispenser outside Baring's bank, the Queen exclaims: 'That's funny, Philip. I thought I had a few bob left in this bank.'

He upset the unions. He upset Ken Livingstone. He sometimes upset his editors, one of whom banned a drawing of Hugh Grant coming down the steps of LAPD to the announcement, 'She swallowed the evidence'. Another asked Jak why he, the cartoonist, was paid more than the editor. 'How many cartoonists have there been and how many editors?' was Jak's reply.

The St Bride's choir under Matthew Morley sang the religious pieces with their usual grace and then let their hair down with an enchanting medley of Jak's favourite standard songs. In the bright October sun outside, the Band of the Welsh Guards saw us off with a stirring couple of the Military Marches dear to the old boy's heart.

In the memorable words of Andrew Wilson: 'He behaved more like a squaddie on 48 hours leave, than as the grand old man of the *Evening Standard*.'

Ecclesiastes 3:1-8
To every thing there is a season, and a time to every purpose under the heaven:
A time to be born, and a time to die; a time to plant, and a time to pluck up that which is planted;
A time to kill, and a time to heal; a time to break down, and a time to build up;
A time to weep, and a time to laugh; a time to mourn, and a time to dance;
A time to cast away stones, and a time to gather stones together; a time to embrace, and a time to refrain from embracing;
A time to get, and a time to lose; a time to keep, and a time to cast away;
A time to rend, and a time to sew; a time to keep silence, and a time to speak;
A time to love, and a time to hate; a time of war, and a time of peace.

Sir Georg Solti, KBE
1912-1997
Westminster Abbey

James Lees-Milne
1908-1997
Grosvenor Chapel, Mayfair, London

THE PRINCE OF WALES, a duke and a duchess, a lady-in-waiting representing her sick princess, an ex-PM and nine ambassadors were present. Five conductors, three priests and a rabbi, two dames, three choirs, two organists and three orchestras, as well as a host of international singing stars, combined to send Sir Georg Solti memorably across the great divide.

The Dean's Bidding was beautifully realised. 'He was a truly international figure. He earned this stature through the one language that transcends the limitations of culture and learning: music. We shall celebrate with words, but, above all, with music – in many cases music for which he had a particular love.'

Two handsome Dames, Diana Rigg and Kiri Te Kanawa, spoke and sang as well as they have ever done (*Revelations* 21 and *Morgen* by Strauss). Both Hans J Bar and Lord Birkett addressed Solti's gift for opening doors for younger musicians. Birkett stressed that 'end of an era' was a singularly inappropriate verdict on the death of one who did so much to foster a continuing of tradition.

Of course, we had Bartók and Kodály – the anthem from his *Missa Brevis*, led by Sarah Walker, Robert Tear and Gwynne Howell. The final chorale from Bach's *St John Passion* – which Solti was preparing at his death – was conducted from his score by Philippe Auguin, ringing out with the combined forces of the Abbey choir, the London Voices and a galaxy of 16 of Sir Georg's illustrious friends.

A FEW WEEKS LATER, in the white and gold Grosvenor Chapel, a beautifully printed order of service and an elegant Bidding by Rev Thomas Gibson, formerly Vicar of Badminton, prepared us for suitably affectionate, stylish tributes to James Lees-Milne. Nigel Nicolson celebrated him warmly. He and Martin Drury emphasised Lees-Milne's lasting memorials: his diaries and the inspiring roll call of great houses he saved for the National Trust. Three lovely anthems threaded the service. The last, Lennox Berkeley's setting of George Herbert's words, 'O that I once past changing were,/Fast in thy Paradise, where no flower can wither!', for a solo voice, was perhaps the most poignant.

The Duchess of Devonshire's choice of extract from Lees-Milne's *Another Self* was inspired. Her face dimpled in infectious amusement as she read of his incongruous army exploits, striking a ready chord in a congregation which surely boasted enough octogenarians to double *The Oldie*'s circulation. How appropriate! James Lees-Milne was a regular reader.

Revelations 21:1-5
And I saw a new heaven and a new earth: for the first heaven and the first earth were passed away; and there was no more sea. And I John saw the holy city, new Jerusalem, coming down from God out of heaven, prepared as a bride adorned for her husband. And I heard a great voice out of heaven saying, Behold, the tabernacle of God is with men, and he will dwell with them, and they shall be his people, and God himself shall be with them, and be their God.

James Villiers
1933-1998

John Wells
1936-1998

Both at St Paul's Church, Covent Garden

RECOLLECTIONS OF JAMES VILLIERS poured from his friends who came to read or speak in his memory. Johnny Kidd recalled his first sighting at Richmond Horse Show. After Harvey Smith had ruined a clear round at the last fence, the tall, elegant figure shook a remonstrating finger at the great rider and intoned, 'Naughty little sausage'. At the end of their first day at RADA, Bryan Pringle asked, 'What are you doing this evening?' 'Going home to dress for dinner. Doesn't everyone?' Jeremy Child listed Jimbo's eccentric use of favourite words, borrowed from his father: 'rare', 'agreeable', 'chambers', 'deeply moving'. James Cellan Jones had sent the actor a script. Silence prompted a call, 'What do you think?', and the languid reply: 'A bit short on the text, luvvie.' Peter O'Toole read from his brilliant account of Jimbo's committal to hospital. He reappeared smartly to join his concerned friends at the bar next door, elegant in pyjamas and dressing-gown. He also reminded us of the Arundel vicar preaching at the funeral who made the felicitous discovery that a correct interpretation of the Aramaic text, 'In my father's house are many mansions', is 'On my father's estate are many taverns.'

I have rarely heard so many speakers evoke a man so warmly and so vividly. His two brothers read his favourite poems and we were treated to the recorded voices of the Ink Spots, Ella Fitzgerald, Richard Burton and Frank Sinatra, backed by Peter Cook, Dudley Moore, Noël Coward and Jimbo himself.

FOR JOHN WELLS' CROWDED memorial celebration two days later I found myself aloft beside the organ. A splendid view, but a difficult acoustic.

Surveying the varied congregation, Richard Ingrams highlighted the diversity of John's interests and acquaintances, 'proved by the fact that I don't know who half of you are.' Remembering Oxford days with Wells – 'We were a gang who had fun and wanted to go on having it for the rest of our lives.' Most fun was 'Mrs Wilson's Diary' and the 'Dear Bill' letters, and if Ingrams did not warm to one of Wells' jokes, he took a leaf out of Robert Morley's book: 'Put it in another play, my darling.' Tom Stoppard quoted the early notoriety – 'Sweet peddling Eton schoolmaster' – and celebrated John's versatility and virtuosity. Lord Runcie forgave the label 'Runcieballs' and reminded us of John's Christian faith.

A Salvation Army band added body to the lusty singing and Kate Flowers, Nuala Willis and Eric Roberts were in fine voice for Offenbach, Handel and Wells/Carl Davis. Dolly Wells and Jim Broadbent read Hardy's *Afterwards* and from *Sentimental Journey*. The theatrical highlight was Edward Fox's imaginative performance of A P Herbert's *Ninth Wicket*, a very funny mimed monologue which he had committed to memory.

Master Beauregard Jagger made several lusty contributions during readings and addresses which John Wells would, we hope, have relished.

Maureen, Marchioness of Dufferin and Ava

1907-1998

St Margaret's Church, Westminster

LORD ST JOHN OF FAWSLEY quoted the Irish poet and songwriter Thomas Moore as his text: 'And from love's shining circle, the gems have passed away.' With such a vivid subject he could equally have explored the same poet's, 'All those endearing young charms' or 'You may break, you may shatter the vase if you will/but the scent of roses will hang round it still.'

Two tubs of pink roses (from the Owl House? From Clandeboye?) along with what looked like the 'Heartsease, Loosestrife, Love-lies-bleeding' quoted elsewhere, decorated the main aisle. Down it, at least 24 Guinnesses walked. Appropriately, many in the congregation wore the elaborate hats beloved by the Marchioness. There was a saucy silver and jet beret and a couple of black velvet hoops nose-diving down the face of a woman who picked her way with delicate uncertainty. The most spectacular were worn by the granddaughters, Evgenia Sands and Ivana Lowell. From my seat, next to the St John's Ambulance lady at the back of the church, one looked like a vast squashed busby and the other a mass of delicate black netting neatly entrapping a cloud of black butterflies.

In light of the famous court battle against her daughters, which the Guinness heiress won, to assert her right to give £15 million directly to her two grandchildren, there was a happy irony in the passage from *I Peter 1*: 3-9 which Ivana Lowell chose to read. It referred to 'the hope of an inheritance', but went on to emphasise that, 'Even gold passes in the assayer's fire, and much more precious than perishable gold is faith which stands the test.'

Mrs Sands read John Betjeman's moving lines from 1944, '*In memory of Basil, Marquess of Dufferin and Ava*.' 'The poet awaits ...your dear return/ with a Bullingdon noise of an evening/In a Sports-Bugatti from Thame/that belonged to a man in Magdalen./Friend of my youth, you are dead!/And the quads are empty without you.'

Lord Dudley's light verse, if not quite as polished, is also celebrated. Bravely, he followed the Betjeman with his *Guinness Was Good for Us*, finishing, 'Be consoled, not down in the dumps/that Maureen's played her final hand/In life her slam was always grand,/and, where she is, she'll turn up trumps.'

Lord St John's measured address eloquently and affectionately covered a long life early in which his subject saw the flames that burnt the Dublin Post Office and, for her last party at Claridges, suggested 'White tie and tiaras'.

Norman promised more of that on the other side, along with trumpets.

1 Peter 1: 3-9
Blessed be the God and Father of our Lord Jesus Christ, which according to his abundant mercy hath begotten us again unto a lively hope by the resurrection of Jesus Christ from the dead, to an inheritance incorruptible, and undefiled, and that fadeth not away, reserved in heaven for you, who are kept by the power of God through faith unto salvation ready to be revealed in the last time. Wherein ye greatly rejoice, though now for a season, if need be, ye are in heaviness through manifold temptations: That the trial of your faith, being much more precious than of gold that perisheth, though it be tried with fire, might be found unto praise and honour and glory at the appearing of Jesus Christ: Whom having not seen, ye love; in whom, though now ye see him *not, yet believing, ye rejoice with joy unspeakable and full of glory: Receiving the end of your faith, even the salvation of your souls.*

Archbishop Trevor Huddleston, CR, KCMG

1913-1998

Westminster Abbey

I SUPPOSE IT WAS unremarkable that such a mass of clergy should assemble, such pools of episcopal purple, such a congregation of shining black faces. Trevor Huddleston's name is inseparable from Africa.

The Abbey's impeccable stage management does not usually incude a warm-up act, but the South African choir and the Manhattan Brothers, later an integral part of the service (*'Farewell, good friend'*), jumped up a couple of times before it started with lively bursts of *a capella* harmonising.

After their second set there was a disturbance in front of the sacrarium. At first I thought it was a street-theatre piece informally celebrating this turbulent priest. (The Bishop of Bath and Wells was later to tell us that Huddleston claimed he was allowed into Sophiatown only because the police understood 'that the clergy are harmless. I tried to alter all that!') I was wrong. This *was* a protest. Moments passed before the Abbey officials were able to hustle the man away. Heaven knows what he was shouting. I thought I heard the word 'Islam!' – but whether he was for it or against it, I could not tell.

My venerable clerical neighbour nodded wisely. 'That was the sort of thing Trevor was used to,' he whispered approvingly. We entered calmer waters with the introit, Vaughan Williams' beguiling, lilting setting of Milton's, 'Nothing is here for tears, nothing to wail'. Then some words by Henry Scott Holland which, for once, had nothing to do with going into the next room. Set to Rhuddlan, a melody from Edward Jones's *Musical Relicks of Welsh Bards*, they started, 'Judge eternal, throned in splendour... purge this realm of bitter things.'

Readings charted Huddleston's progress. From *The True and Living God* came his Christian awakening and the testing of his vocation at Mirfield. The Lesson from St Luke proclaimed, 'Let the oppressed go free.' Nelson Mandela's message recalled the Archbishop's frustrated cry, 'Words! Words! Words! I'm sick of words!'

The ANC's Freedom Charter was followed by extracts from *Naught for Your Comfort* and *Return to South Africa: The Ecstasy and the Agony*, with the sobering 1991 message, 'Optimism, like patriotism, is not enough. But hope is enough because it is based on realism.'

Most moving was the noble solo trumpet improvisation by the great Hugh Masekela who, said Bishop Jim, got his first instrument from the Archbishop, 'to the immediate discomfort of his neighbours'.

Jim Thompson followed Trevor Huddleston into the Diocese of Stepney. Before he left some 13 years later, whenever he was introduced as Bishop of Stepney people said, 'Isn't that Trevor Huddleston?'

Extract from Samson Agonistes (Milton)
Nothing is here for tears, nothing to wail
Or knock the breast, no weakness, no contempt,
Dispraise, or blame, nothing but well and fair,
And what may quiet us in a death so noble.

Sir David English

1931-1998

St Martin-in-the-Fields

IT WAS STRANGE WATCHING Keith Waterhouse in the opposite gallery. Fleet Street and Westminster were saying farewell to David English, and Waterhouse and I have been touring a highly successful try-out of his new play *Good Grief* which begins after a Fleet Street editor's memorial service.

The fiction takes place at St Bride's, but Sir David was too big a draw and Canon Oates and his versatile choir came on a day transfer to Trafalgar Square. The vainglorious choices made by Waterhouse's editor were missing. No *My Way*, no *We'll Meet Again*, no nipping into the next room with Canon Henry Holland. Only *He Who Would Valiant Be* and *Onward, Christian Soldiers* survived among hardy memorial perennials.

The service was characterised by a series of simple readings by the family and Sir David's long-time personal secretary, Ina. A constant theme was his devotion to his widow, Irene, whom he was nursing through Alzheimer's.

Stewart Steven touched vividly on this and relished a vintage collection of anecdotes. The kipper nailed under the schoolmaster's desk; the mailbag stolen from Paddington Station to authenticate the story of a security lapse for the *Mirror*; the subsequent plea to the magistrate threatening a custodial sentence, 'I'm getting married in the morning'; the wedding brought forward two months to authenticate this; the honeymoon spent with the best man as the bride could not change her diary; the trip to China when English, challenged with a single duck's head on a silver platter, bravely munched through it under the mistaken impression that protocol required it.

St Bride's choir was on top form with Mozart, Stanford, the Stainer Sevenfold Amen, and a selection from Cole Porter's *High Society*. Don

Lusher's Big Band, which had accompanied Sheila Southern on a charming *You Make Me Feel So Young*, blasted us out into the Charing Cross Road.

Just as at Trevor Huddleston's thanksgiving at the Abbey, there was a silly political demonstration. The faces of Lady Thatcher, Tony Blair and William Hague froze as the offenders were hustled away. Bodyguards fingered their guns and let the church staff get on with it.

Derek Robert Nimmo

1930-1999

St Paul's Church, Covent Garden

HOWEVER MUCH WE MAY regret the laughs Derek Nimmo will not give us in the future, we could not have laughed more readily or warmly at his memorial service.

His grandchildren called him 'Gumpy', and Charlie, aged four, had labelled this 'Gumpy's Happy Service'. Charlie also contributed a song about a clown, 'Ha! Ha! Ha! Ho! Ho! Ho!', and nearly blew the microphone away with a first blast which brought siblings and relatives rushing to reposition it. Florence (seven) had a word of warning for God: 'He likes very good wine and also showing people around the place and he likes having lots of dinner parties and telling people where to sit.' George, several years older, was just as moving.

Canon John Hester thanked Nimmo 'on behalf of the clerical profession for his contribution to their image.'

Gerald Starper's Tribute cited Derek's resolve to 'live life outrageously', with the vital caveat, 'if you can carry it off'. He brought a new dimension to the art of the actor-manager with his Far East tours: 'Hong Kong is much more fun than Birmingham.'

Geoffrey Palmer's perfectly pitched *Recollections* started with a first meeting with Nimmo as a children's TV chimpanzee emerging from the sewers to terrorise Battersea. 'The least convincing performance that I shall ever see.' Twenty-five years later he reluctantly agreed to meet the actor-manager in a lay-by on the A40. 'I shall be in a yellow Ford – in case I don't recognise you,' he gamesmanned. 'What will you be driving?' 'I shall be in a coffee and cream Rolls Royce,' was the winning reply. More seriously, he emphasised Derek's memory for and politeness to hotel staff, his generosity in casting and his knowledge of the countries he visited. 'Is it safe to eat?' (of street food) 'They've been eating it here for hundreds of years.' From Nimmo he had 'learnt how to live.'

Maureen Lipman, always 'Lipman' to his 'Lord Nimmo', sang *I Like Life*. 'I have to do it like Joyce Grenfell, or I shan't get through it.'

Clement Freud, with Tribute and Recollections already spoken for, settled for Address. 'I can't remember when I met him. I can't remember if...!' Like many of us, Sir Clement had queried the coat of arms on the buttons decorating the cloak which often enveloped Derek's uniquely grand chauffeur. 'Your coat of arms?' Freud once asked. 'No, the chauffeur's.'

Like all the others, he saluted Patricia Nimmo and her husband's assertion that he couldn't possibly be all that bad if such a paragon had put up with him for so long.

'With all my love for ever and ever, Amen,' was her note on the last page of the Order of Service.

The Right Honourable The Lord Denning, OM

1899-1999

Westminster Abbey

HOW MANY TIMES HAVE I heard at fashionable first nights the suggestion that if a bomb fell on the building it would be the end of the British theatre? If that bomb had dropped on Westminster Abbey on Thursday, 16 June, the obliteration of the legal profession would have been complete.

The Lord High Chancellor, the Master of the Rolls, the Lord Chief Justice, the Lord Chief Justice of Northern Ireland, the President of the Family Division, the Vice Chancellor of the Supreme Court, many Lords of Appeal, 25 Lord Justices, 26 Mr Justices, 13 His Honours, 15 Judges, 75 QCs and the representatives of innumerable legal societies, all wiped out along with your reviewer (barrister-at-law).

Reading *Sonnet 30*, Lord Denning's stepdaughter, Lady Hazel Fox, acknowledged its legal imagery ('sessions', 'summons', 'grievances', 'account') but emphasised the last two lines: 'But if the while I think on thee, dear friend/All losses are restor'd and sorrows end.'

In the Bidding, the Dean 'Remembered with thanksgiving a legal legend... the mightier a figure this Hampshire man became, the more he seemed instinctively to grasp the world of ordinary citizens.'

Professor Robert Denning read the peroration from the address given by his father at Norwich Cathedral in 1982. The Lord Chief Justice Lord Bingham's wide-ranging Address considered the centenarian 'the best known and best loved judge in the history of the law' with 'a unique gift of human warmth'. He had 'a proper respect for authority but not the authorities.' He quoted Lord Devlin on Denning's career – always innovative even if he was occasionally over-ruled. 'When Tom and I were young, the Common Law had gone into a decline... He opened a door to the law above the law.'

He quoted several of Denning's characteristic, homely summations: 'It was bluebell time in Kent...'; 'Old Herbert Bundy of Broadchalke had only one asset, a farm which had been in his family for 300 years. He did a very foolish thing. He mortgaged it to the bank...'

Best was Denning's reply when a much younger Bingham cited a precedent established by Lord Simon and six other Lords of Appeal. 'Lord Simon was very sorry he said that. He told me so.'

A simple and great thanksgiving service for a great and simple man.

Sonnet 30 *(William Shakespeare)*
When to the sessions of sweet silent thought
I summon up remembrance of things past,
I sigh the lack of many a thing I sought,
And with old woes new wail my dear time's waste:
Then can I drown an eye, unused to flow,
For precious friends hid in death's dateless night,
And weep afresh love's long since cancell'd woe,
And moan the expense of many a vanish'd sight:
Then can I grieve at grievances foregone,
And heavily from woe to woe tell o'er
The sad account of fore-bemoanèd moan,
Which I new pay as if not paid before.
But if the while I think on thee, dear friend,
All losses are restored and sorrows end.

Charles Wintour

1917-1999

Floral Hall, Royal Opera House

I OWE MY FIRST glimpse of the new Covent Garden complex to Charles Wintour's request for a secular celebration of his life. Very handsome it all looked, and so did the Great and the Good who turned out on a wet Monday morning.

The *Evening Standard*'s former Editor's daughter, Anna, tackled the charge of 'Chilly Charlie' head-on. Not to his family – shy, perhaps, hesitant about telling his son the facts of life, romantic and prone to old-fashioned expressions of surprise ('I say!') and disapproval ('Fast set'). She reminded us of a regular joke at the *Evening Standard* Awards, where Tom Stoppard, as so often, wins a prize. Young Stoppard asked Wintour for a job. His CV declared an interest in politics. The Editor asked him who the Home Secretary was. 'I said I was interested,' Stoppard replied. 'I didn't say I was obsessed.'

An erstwhile Home Secretary, Roy Jenkins, praised Wintour's detachment, which enabled him to be politically alert and in touch but uncompromised, and to keep his distance in handling his mischievous proprietor, Lord Beaverbrook.

Charles Wintour's passion for theatre produced Harold Pinter, who read from *The Caretaker*. A dramatic critic might suggest that he read it too quickly. The odd pause would have been telling. In a charming interlude, three of Wintour's grandchildren – two with pronounced American voices, one in bell-like English tones– read Dylan Thomas' *Do Not Go Gentle*.

Max Hastings spoke of the debt he owed to Wintour, 'shamelessly elitist, shy, but never cold.' When he asked his Editor to send him to cover a war in the Middle East, he was dismissed as 'the least qualified person of the five' who had applied that day. It had to be worked for.

Arthur Schlesinger, still 'Junior' 34 years after his father's death, met Wintour, then Editor of *Granta*, at Peterhouse in 1938. Schlesinger returned a copy of the magazine with a sheaf of notes setting out its 'manifold shortcomings'. A lifelong friendship followed.

A quintet from the orchestra of the Royal Opera House played Beethoven and Schubert. On leaving, Sir Robin Day expressed a wish for the more robust *When the Saints Go Marching In* at his memorial service, which we all hope will be a long time ahead.

The Rt Hon Alan Kenneth McKenzie Clark, MP

1925-1999

St Margaret's Church, Westminster Abbey

THE GREAT AND THE GOOD were out in force for Alan Clark – overshadowed only by the dignified ushers of St Margaret's who, as always, looked even Greater and even Better.

'The Lady' was abroad but her consort, Denis, was in affable form. 'The man who bought his own furniture' was absent, but the coiner of the phrase appropriated by Clark was there. There was no sign of he of the strategically placed corncob, or he who was unaware that 'we dress for dinner at Saltwood on Fridays'; nor was 'the lovely little Brummie accent' which once pointed out signs of intoxication in the House of Commons to be heard. We looked in vain for the colleague described as 'indecisive, blustering, bullying, stupid and cunningly cautious', though many present might have claimed the label. Of the two Normans, one still 'radiated menace' and the other, 'little Norman', can no longer carry off the adjective 'Mephistophelean'.

But to the Service of Thanksgiving, which, let's face it, was why we were there. The Bidding said it all: 'Politician, historian, writer', 'spirited independence', 'readiness to take risks', 'patriot', 'beloved Highlands', 'respect for God's creatures.'

The hymns were sung lustily to good, forthright tunes: Vaughan Williams, Parry, and Hughes' *'Cwm Rhondda'*. Alan's son, Andrew Clark, read from Mark 4: 'Let us pass over to the other side', and his kilted brother James delivered a fiercely passionate attack on Wilfred Owen's *'Anthem for Doomed Youth'*: 'What passing-bells for these who die as cattle?/Only the monstrous anger of the guns', which powerfully evoked Clark's *'Donkeys'*, one of the inspirations for *'O What a Lovely War'*.

This was in marked contrast to the gentle melancholy of George Butterworth's setting for the famous lines from Housman's *A Shropshire Lad* – 'Loveliest of trees, the cherry now', beautifully sung by Paul Charrier.

Euan Graham's address marked the second occasion on which he has spoken for Alan Clark. They met at Oxford in the coffee shop opposite Balliol. Clark had lost his driving licence 'for the relatively trivial offence of allowing a girl to drive his car sitting on his lap while he controlled the pedals with his feet.' The 'gleaming Buick' took the new friends to Gloucestershire. Graham, a Clerk to the House of Lords, introduced the fledgling MP to all the bars in the Palace of Westminster. 'He took to it like a duck to water.' He closed with 'They told me, Heraclitus, they told me you were dead', an excellent piece for memorial services by William Cory, who also gave us *Jolly boating weather?*

Heraclitus *(William Cory)*
They told me, Heraclitus, they told me you were dead,
They brought me bitter news to hear and bitter tears to shed.
I wept as I remember'd how often you and I
Had tired the sun with talking and sent him down the sky.

And now that thou art lying, my dear old Carian guest,
A handful of grey ashes, long, long ago at rest,
Still are thy pleasant voices, thy nightingales, awake;
For Death, he taketh all away, but them he cannot take.

Lt Col Sir Harry Llewellyn

1911-1999

St Luke's Church, Chelsea

THE LLEWELLYN CLAN CHOSE the church in which Dickens was married
to celebrate their patriarch's life. The church where Surtees was wed might
have been more appropriate, but your critic could not have told them where
to find it and the high, handsome St Luke's easily accommodated the large
crowd of family and friends, many from Wales, and most glowing with the
ruddy health of the shires.

Sir Harry's wife 'Teeny' died before him, and Roddy Llewellyn dedicated
to her his reading from G J Whyte Melville's *Riding Recollections*. Lady
Llewellyn, her son remembered, had broken some 90 bones during her life.
The author warned a young woman that 'her less muscular frame is more
easily injured than a man's.' Too late!

Roddy's brother Dai, now dignified, but perhaps not yet redeemed,
as Sir David Llewellyn, Bt, read Ronald Duncan's *In Praise of the Horse*,
familiar from the last day of the Horse of the Year Show. He prefaced it with
a letter from 'a good address in Hampshire' topped by 'a handsome crest',
thanking Sir Harry personally for the invitation to his Memorial Service and
apologising for the writer's inability to attend.

Douglas Bunn, Master of Hickstead, first met Sir Harry 54 years ago when
they competed in the Victory Championships at White City. Llewellyn
was 36, Bunn 18. As one of the two finalists with clear rounds Bunn was
winning the jump-off until he made a mess of the last fence, ceding victory
to Llewellyn's determination on 'a good but not a great horse'.

We heard the famous names, Foxhunter, Mr Softy, Stroller; of the
puissance specialist, never happier than with a fence six or seven feet high;
of a dramatic recovery at the Helsinki Games; of inspiring *chef d'équipery*

in Mexico; and of the birth, not the rebirth, of show-jumping after the war, uniting the civilian and the military strands.

We heard of a life saved from the River Usk; of an expert nature photographer; of a disregard for laundry and the bath. We heard of war service with Montgomery from El Alamein to the Rhine. Sir Harry only admitted to 'pitching Monty's tent', but must have done more to earn his Mention in Despatches.

Douglas Bunn found it difficult but essential to mention Sir Harry's reluctance to part with money, reckoning the word 'skinflint' inappropriate in a eulogy. However, he made a happy comparison with Jack Benny and the comforting reflection that Sir Harry's heirs would certainly prefer the saving to the squandering of their inheritance.

In Praise of the Horse (*Ronald Duncan*)
Where in this wide world can man find nobility without pride,
friendship without envy, or beauty without vanity?
Here where grace is laced with muscle and strength by gentleness confined.

He serves without servility; he has fought without enmity.
There is nothing so powerful, nothing less violent;
there is nothing so quick, nothing more patient.

England's past has been borne on his back.
All our history is in his industry.
We are his heirs;
He is our inheritance

Ladies and Gentlemen – the Horse!

Peter Chad Tigar Levi

1931-2000

St Mary the Virgin, Oxford

I HAD NOT BEEN into the University church for nearly 50 years until the beautifully judged service for Peter Levi. There was a sad irony as the train bowled me through a sunny Thames Valley. The *Evening Standard* listed Peter among those celebrating birthdays on 16 May, but I was on my way to celebrate his life in a congregation of poets and academics.

The hymns were vigorous. The music lovely. Georgina Wilson and the choir were followed by Vaughan Williams' *The Lark Ascending*, hauntingly played by Mila Moustakova, accompanied by Matthew Halls, St Mary's organist.

Peter was above all a poet, and Deirdre Levi had chosen two friends to read three of his poems each. Peter Jay read verses from three decades, *The Uccello Canary*, *Cathedrals* and the resonant late-'70s' *Stone on Stone on Stone*.

David Pryce-Jones' eulogy was a model of wit and sympathetic appreciation. He ranged over Peter's endearing qualities – teaching his Stonyhurst pupils to sing '*Il est cocu le chef de gare*' out of the train window as they arrived in the Auvergne; defining a scholar as 'a man who claims to know more about an obscure subject than the only other man to make the same claim.' He wrote his last letter to Pryce-Jones himself, just before he died, in the large hieroglyphics of his blindness. In it he warmly acknowledged his debt to and affection for Alan Pryce-Jones, who had just died at a great age.

David Enders

1922-2000

Chelsea Old Church

CHELSEA OLD CHURCH IS my parish church. Its choir (Director of Music, Andrea Watson) also rose to the occasion to celebrate one of the most faithful members of its congregation. I hadn't been to a similar service there since the funeral of David Enders' long-time companion, John Glen, many years ago. Both were actors and later restaurateurs (the '60s' L'Aiglon in Old Church Street and later the Chichester Festival Restaurant). David's fame came from his starring roles for BBC Radio Drama in its heyday.

He was a devoted Chelsean. I used to meet him of a morning zealously removing lewd calling cards from King's Road phone boxes. (Who has the mantle?)

Lord Cadogan read from *Pilgrim's Progress*. David's plumber recalled coming upon him in his kitchen in Carlyle Square entertaining a dustman who laughed immodestly as Dame Edith Evans chatted and darned a sock in another corner.

A younger brother, Peter Enders, affectionately evoked his sibling as a smart young '30s' figure and suggested that, at Heaven's Gate, St Peter would not send down a harsh sentence but perhaps a short spell of community service, 'for vanity'.

in Scott

1920-2000

Church, Covent Garden

USES St James', Piccadilly, or All Saints, Langham ... departed; but for Robin Scott they opted for the Actors' ... new parish priest, Mark Oakley, who has settled in nicely. Perhaps inspired by the presence of Sir David Attenborough, he emphasised Robin's position at the top of his profession in the Bidding by recalling the old Danish proverb (new to me), '*The higher the monkey climbs the more you can see of his bottom*'.

Sir Paul Fox denied himself such colourful metaphor, sticking to the distinguished career: Bryanston, Cambridge, outside broadcasts, BBC man in Paris, BBC 2, retirement, rebirth, LWT, opera and ballet, the Scala, the Met, flowers, wine and the Garrick.

The French connection was emphasised by Philippe Bacon with a delightful passage from *Les Silences du Colonel Bramble* by André Maurois. M. Bacon read in French, but asked us not to follow the translation lest we got the jokes too soon. I think we laughed at the right times. I hope we did.

Douglas Fairbanks Jnr

1909-2000

St Martin-in-the-Fields

SOME NEWS PAGES HAVE commented snidely on the attendance at Douglas Fairbanks' celebration – still Jnr, even in death – but at 91 you are likely to have lost many friends and contemporaries and some 200 souls attended, including a duke, a duchess, three earls and three countesses.

Sir Anthony Acland, who met Fairbanks in Washington, recalled his war service with Combined Ops, 'A hell of a war', and his honorary knighthood for fostering Anglo-American relations. Jeremy Clyde and his two brothers remembered when their father, Sir Tommy, and Fairbanks were film-producing partners. Jeremy spoke movingly of the actor's heartwarming, one-sided, transatlantic phone call when his father lay on his deathbed.

All emphasised his exquisite pre-war manners and his irresistible charm. I can testify to this. I interviewed him once for radio and he characterised at least 17 people whose names I raised with one word: 'charming' – even his first wife, Joan Crawford. Of Marlene Dietrich, with whom he had a famous affair, he for once added 'and she was an excellent cook'.

The choir of St Bride's was guesting, offering a lovely *Londonderry Air* to augment Fauré's *In Paradisum* and the *Cantique de Jean Racine*.

André Deutsch

1917-2000

Stationers' Hall, London EC4

ANDRÉ DEUTSCH LEFT NO instructions for a Memorial Service apart from hoping that there would be a party. So a 'meeting' was arranged at Stationers' Hall.

I confess that on these occasions I like a couple of rousing hymns and a prayer or two; but the publishing throng, plump suits and dusty ladies, gathered together on Monday, 16 October, a date conveniently chosen to coincide with the Frankfurt Book Fair, seemed happy to meet and reminisce and then to move to another room to enjoy Paul Hamlyn's hospitality.

I was inescapably reminded of a well-heeled crowd in the opening scenes of a P D James novel, and half-expected a murder to crown the proceedings.

Graham C Greene was a genial Master of Ceremonies, first introducing Penny Buckland, a long-suffering PA who had worked at Deutsch, gone to America and bravely returned. She read a cherished letter found among her employer's papers. It was from an Australian librarian whom the publisher had befriended many years before when she was a very young girl. She had subsequently watched his career with admiration from afar.

Peter Mayer, who had flown in from America en route to Frankfurt, remembered the elderly Deutsch forgetting not one but two celebratory lunches at the Gay Hussar. For Deutsch, he felt, not to be able to publish books he wanted to publish and having to publish books he didn't like would be agony in the contemporary, conglomerate world.

Your editor was slyly introduced by Greene as having given André Deutsch a valued entrée into the Establishment through his association with *Private Eye*. Ingrams recalled presenting his book, *God's Apology*, to the publisher in 1977 and watching him solemnly weigh it, 'like a fishmonger sizing up a slab of cod'. He relished the *Eye*'s link with Deutsch, and reckoned that for quite a time the firm's fortunes depended on Denis Thatcher's 'Dear Bill' letters and *Postman Pat*. Two themes were emerging: Deutsch's parsimony and a general feeling that the fun had gone out of publishing and that small is beautiful.

Tom Wallace, another American, met André Deutsch and adopted him as a surrogate father when his own Viennese father died in 1960. He looked forward to retracing the steps they had taken through the German rooms at the Book Fair in 1961.

Very much the queen of the show was Diana Athill, basking in the success of her recent memoir, *Stet*. She reminisced about Saturdays with volunteer staff members spending their time on the office floor stuffing promotional envelopes under the enthusiastic tuition of their economising boss.

She read an appreciative letter from John Updike, an author who had stayed faithful, and pointed out some examples of fiction-writer's licence in it. He struck the final note of economical management by confessing that André Deutsch had taught him how to extract staples from a book envelope in order to use them again.

Desmond Wilcox

1931-2000

St Martin-in-the-Fields

WERE I TO LIST all the contributors to Desmond Wilcox's Memorial Service it would challenge comparison with the cast of a Royal Variety Show, the contents of a popular anthology and the index to *Palgrave's Golden Treasury*. The Widow Wilcox was not going to let her man down – wisely, she allowed two hours. Greg Dyke still had to creep out before the end.

Inside, the Order of Service was Ken Pyne's caricature of Desmond at the Golden Gates (not a pearl in sight), fearlessly thrusting his microphone forward and asking, 'God, how does it feel...?' There were readings by many admirably composed Wilcox children; Nerys Hughes did Masefield; Michael Parkinson did Parkinson; Marti Webb, Black and Lloyd Webber; Stilgoe did Stilgoe; Maureen Lipman, Rupert Brooke; June Whitfield, Keith Waterhouse; Terry Wogan did St Paul.

Musical splendours were provided by the Woodfalls Concert Brass (President D Wilcox). A cousin from Australia, Kate Taylor, sang *She Moved Through the Fair*, a song with which Esther had wooed her husband. The African Children's Choir had the whole world in their hands, and Cleo Laine and John Dankworth delivered a sublime *September Song*.

Before the Sherma, Rabbi David Goldberg spoke affectionately of Desmond's enthusiastic conversion and his keenness, if necessary, 'to suffer circumcision with a blunt instrument'. Colin Morris, a Methodist minister who could sell Fox's Glacier Mints to polar bears, emphasised the ecumenical aspects of the service; Desmond's virtuosity in filling in T & D expenses forms; his kamikaze questions at BBC TV production Review Boards, and the artistic rows that penetrated the walls of their adjoining BBC offices – so loud that one bustle of bishops had to be persuaded it was overhearing a rehearsal of a Dennis Potter play.

The passionate conflicts of husband and wife reminded the parson of

'Africa and two charging rhinos'. However, he knew – and we knew – that they represented a secure affection.

David Jackson, the South American boy whose face rebuilding Desmond watched and recorded with such concern, spoke simply of his debt. We observed a minute's silence for Damilola Taylor, remembered across London at the same time.

She Moved Through the Fair *(Irish folk song)*
My love said to me
My mother won't mind
And me Father won't slight you
For your lack of kind
Then she stepped away from me
And this she did say
It will not be long, love
Till our wedding day.

...The people were saying
No two e'er were wed
But one has a sorrow
That never was said
And she smiled as she passed me
With her goods and her gear
And that was the last
That I saw of my dear.

Godfrey Talbot, LVO, OBE

1908-2000

St Bride's Church, Fleet Street

YOUR CRITIC HAD NOT visited St Bride's since Canon John Oates retired after presiding over George Elrick's memorial service. Canon David Meara is now in confident charge and the choir remains in excellent voice. For Godfrey Talbot, we did not hear their impressive show-tune repertoire; but they did add 'Almighty God' from the finale of Act I of *Aida* to a couple of Parry settings, Orlando Gibbons's *Nunc Dimittis* and some fierce descants in the hymns.

Talbot's 15 or so years as the BBC's Court Correspondent (a title he disliked, considering himself no courtier) were recognised by three representatives of the royal family. Ronald Allison, who succeeded him and went on to be the Queen's Press Secretary, turned out for HM and the Duke of Edinburgh, and gave the address.

Talbot was retired by the BBC at 60 – ironically, only two thirds of the way through his long life. He produced a popular biography of the Queen Mother in 1978, only just over three quarters of the way through hers; and continued to broadcast for LBC. He showed Allison around the various royal premises, invariably welcomed affectionately by the staff. One morning when they were due to visit Clarence House, Allison said he hoped they might be offered coffee. Talbot did not think it likely. 'I shall be very disappointed if we are,' he said.

Godfrey Talbot's finest hour was as a war correspondent with the elite BBC team of Richard Dimbleby, Frank Gillard and Wynford Vaughan Thomas, of which he was the last survivor – 56 years after he reported the news of Montgomery's victory at El Alamein, Reginald Turnill, another old BBC hand, recalled Talbot's vivid way with an expenses form: 'For pulling vehicle out of mud... Drinks to King of Italy... Gratuity to Nun for special services...'

Jonathan Talbot read the usual verses i[...]
grandfather's addiction to gadgetry (anythi[...]
knob to twiddle), his penchant for limericks an[...]
'I think we've heard quite enough, Godfrey.'

Raymond Baxter also revisited the 'Golden Age[...]
Not Stand at My Grave and Weep', attributing its auth[...]
soldier on whose body it was found in Northern Ir[...]
Remembrance, the anthology of material suitable for r[...] [...]es
published by Cruse, it is credited to an anonymous Americ[...] [...]n poet.
The translation is slightly less flowery but the message is the same.

Do Not Stand at My Grave and Weep (Anon)
Do not stand at my grave and weep;
I am not there – I do not sleep.
I am a thousand winds that blow.
I am the diamond glints on snow.
I am the sunlight on ripened grain.
I am the gentle autumn rain.
When you awaken in the morning's hush
I am the swift uplifting rush
Of quiet birds, in circled flight.
I am the soft stars that shine at night.
Do not stand at my grave and cry;
I am not there – I did not die.

The Lord Cowdrey of Tonbridge, CBE

1932-2000

Westminster Abbey

WHILE THE ABBEY LAID on its accustomed personal pomp and civilised ceremony (a parade of the three young captains of Cowdrey's tyro teams proudly leading the Kent County Championship team of 1970 and representatives of the 10 cricketing nations, including Gary Sobers), three items stood out.

Cowdrey's eldest son, Christopher, delivered a model 'Appreciation from the Family', which was both affectionate and witty. 'Why have they all come to London on a Friday?' he imagined his modest father saying; and remembered, as a boy, querying the quixotic decision to fly to Perth to face Thompson at the age of 42. 'I think it'll be rather fun.' ('I don't think we've met, my name is Cowdrey.') He recalled his first visit to Lord's, aged about six, led in by the Grace gate, through the Long Room and out on to the sacred turf for an infant's-eye view. It occurred to him that, as his father's initials were MCC, 'One day all this might be mine.'

He compared his father's ability to ease a ball elegantly through the covers with his brother Graham's inclination to hoist a similar delivery over mid-wicket for six.

After William Douglas-Home's *Cricket's a glorious game, say we/And cricket will live to eternity*, the equivalent of Canon Henry Holland for the Great Game, Tim Rice penned a splendid parody of two Gilbert and Sullivan numbers for Richard Stuart and the choir.

At George Carman's recent do, Gilbert's *Lord Chancellor's Song* could have done with an update. For Cowdrey, Sir Tim supplied an acutely topical 'little list': 'Coaches who would rather run 10 miles than hold a net... chaps whose innings end because some blighter placed a bet... and running with Sir Geoffrey... Young Boycs is on my list... And the off-the-field sensation-seeking tabloid journalist... I don't think he'll be missed... and then there is the batsman who will never walk, alas... unless at least three stumps have been uprooted from the grass... I think you've got the gist... And sons who think mid-wicket is the only place to aim/But then perhaps I'm lucky that they loved the greatest game... In a gesture nepotist...' He left them off the list, together with his adored grandchildren who were all on parade.

The third graceful tribute came from John Major, cricket's preferred eulogist. He highlighted Colin's affinity with the young, his excitement when one of his second wife's horses won a race – 'after a while even the horse got some credit' – and, most revealing, his role as an agony uncle when a beleaguered Prime Minister was holed up in the bunker and No 10. Colin, a compulsive communicator, would write, telephone or turn up smiling over a glass of whisky 'in times of political difficulty...' (nicely judged pause) '...so we talked quite a lot!'

Leslie Edwards, OBE

1915-2001

St Paul's Church, Covent Garden

MARK OAKLEY CONDUCTED LESLIE Edwards' funeral service as well as this memorial and reminded us in the Bidding that on the earlier occasion in February, 'There was a celebration aching to get out.'

The Order of Service reproduced the splendid photograph of the much-loved dancer as Cattalabutte, grandly taking up the curtain at the Opera House when the Royal Ballet reopened it after the war with *The Sleeping Beauty*.

Leslie had completed an unpublished autobiography, *In Good Company*, and Sir Peter Wright read three passages from it. He admitted that the first was 'rather long', but declined to cut it as 'it was all so Leslie'. It recalled his last day with the Royal Ballet in 1993. He awoke feeling that leaving made the day 'Black Monday'; but a Royal Gala gave a sense of occasion to his last appearance as the Prince of Verona in Macmillan's *Romeo and Juliet*, followed by speeches, presentations, a cake, a celebratory meal and a triumphant progress home. 'Black Monday, my foot!'

Another extract confessed his disappointment when he heard that his role at the reopening would be the non-dancing Cattalabutte, and Robert Helpman's brusque response: 'Well, at least you're in it! Why don't you make something of it?' And indeed he did.

Edwards was the devoted founder-director of the Royal Ballet Choreographic School. It was appropriate that two of his most successful protégés, Michael Corder and David Bintley, paid tribute.

Bintley remembered an annual display when his mentor badgered him to supply a ballet. Under pressure, he went into a rehearsal room with a colleague and after an hour produced a one-and-a-half-minute dance called *Minstrels*. As all the other pieces were too long and too worthy, he stole the show. Sir Frederic Ashton's congratulations were qualified by a wistful, 'It could have been a *little* longer.'

Phyllida Ritter spoke for the Friends of Covent Garden, where again Leslie was a popular driving force, on occasion recruiting the majestic Sgt Martin, monarch of the foyer, as Brünnhilde in the climactic tableau of the Christmas concert.

Bintley revisited the cliché, 'No small parts only small players', and freshened it by insisting that Leslie's 70 roles over 60 years made him 'a very big player indeed'.

Sir Anthony Dowell and Antony Twiner performed an interlude from Lord Berners' *A Wedding Bouquet*, a favourite of Leslie's.

The second hymn, *Come to us, Creative Spirit*, is new to me, but is an appropriate discovery for arts memorials.

Come to us, Creative Spirit *(David Mowbray)*
Come to us, Creative Spirit,
In our Father's house...
Poet, painter, music-maker,
All your treasures bring;
Craftsman, actor, graceful dancer
Make your offering...

Elizabeth Kenward, MBE

1906-2001

Guards Chapel, Wellington Barracks

IT WAS UNFAIR THAT reports of the Service of Thanksgiving for Betty Kenward ('the original Jennifer') were ousted from the columns of the *Times* and the *Daily Telegraph* by services for a tradesman (Lord Sieff of Brompton) at the West London Synagogue and a broadcaster (Andrew Mulligan) at Chelsea Old Church.

However, Mrs Kenward would have approved of the large, well-dressed congregation which came to remember her in what she might have described as 'our dear Guards Chapel'. I had thought to thread this report with some of her characteristic lists and phrases – 'Also looking radiant were...', etc, – but I do not have her rare talent for remembering rosters of names without taking a note. So I, too, am confounded by the absence of reports.

The choice of the Guards Chapel was poignant. When it was bombed one Sunday morning, George Kemp-Welch, one of Mrs Kenward's twin brothers, was among those who perished. Of the original building, only the richly decorated Neo-Byzantine apse remains, its beauty emphasised by the severe simplicity of the reconstruction and the red clouds of Guards Colours hanging from the ceiling.

The Band of the Coldstream Guards provided a rousing accompaniment both to the congregation and to the Guards Chapel Choir – especially as they drove each familiar hymn to a thundering conclusion.

I Was Glad and *How Lovely Are Thy Dwellings* were the two Anthems. Two grandchildren, Lucy and Sophie Kenward, gave charming recitations in confident American accents.

Sir Thomas Pilkington spoke the eulogy. Only last December he dined with Mrs Kenward in a noisy restaurant. She chose the one quiet moment to ask, 'You will make the Address at my Memorial Service, won't you?'

He sketched her unhappy childhood; her mother's coldness; running away from home at 16; her pioneering role as a single parent; unlikely war work in an engineering factory; joining *Tatler* in 1944; organising fashion shows during V-bomb raids ('Don't fall on your faces, girls, the clothes are on loan'); 47 glory years as Jennifer; her dislike of photographers and journalists; her tactful description of an unsuccessful party – 'plenty of room to move about'; her racing friends; how she would have hated modern 'so-called celebrities and personalities – goodness knows how they became so!'; and her epic journey from the Windsor Royal Horse Show by Concorde to Caracas via Paris and back on the return flight.

A piece of risqué verse was found in her bag after her death – the one which begins, 'In Brighton she was Brenda...' and ends, '...and down on his expenses she was petrol, oil and lunch.' It wasn't clear if Sir Thomas thought she was the author. We can reassure him that she was not.

Brian Dominic Frederick Titus Leo Brindley

1935-2001

St Etheldreda's, Holborn

BRIAN BRINDLEY'S DEATH DURING an eight-course banquet at the Athenaeum two days short of his 70th birthday abruptly ended his months of planning and received wider covering in the public prints than he might have expected. Less would have disappointed him.

'Dominic' and 'Titus' were names he added to his baptismal quota; 'Leo' he adopted when he was confirmed into the Catholic Church. Fittingly he had asked for 'the Solemn Mass of Requiem' to be offered for his soul at St Ethelreda's, which, I understand, is the oldest Catholic parish church in London. It can rarely have been more crowded to overflow. The brief of these reviews is to report Memorial Services, but I think Brian's Memorial will be this Mass. The coffin was brought into the church on the previous day at the end of the Mass of the Assumption and 'reposed overnight in the House of God'. One of his obituarists recorded that, although throughout his life he rarely talked about God, 'he did, however, have an absolutely secure faith in the truth of the Christian religion'.

'Nothing can come between us and the love of Christ' (*Romans* 8:1) was the burden of Alan Bennett's second reading. The first was from Isaiah. I do not know if Brian planned it – he planned most things. It aptly recalled the banquet he had famously prepared, dying, as Damian Thomas recorded in the *Spectator*, 'between the 'Drest' crab and the *Boeuf en Croûte*'. 'On this mountain, Jahweh Sabaoth will prepare for all peoples a banquet of rich food, a banquet of fine wines, of food rich and juicy, of fine, strained wines.'

One piece of planning defeated Brian. Traffic delayed his chosen celebrant Fr Sean Finnegan's attempt to get to Holborn. The Rector, Fr Kit Cunningham, a reassuring presence and an old hand, stepped in.

Paul Gillham, St Ethelreda's Master of Music, had lavished care on Maurice Duruflé's *Messe des Morts*, Brian's choice. He was a great enthusiast for plain-song; he translated and prepared much church music.

Fr Anthony Symondson, who pronounced Brian's absolution at the Athenaeum, preached the Homily, neatly catching his subject's 'Mediterranean' attitude to religion, 'hot, not cold'; his happy childhood, his years at Stowe School and Exeter College, his wonderful work as vicar of Holy Trinity, Oxford Road, Reading; his Synod politics and his 'fall'. He made an arresting comparison with the intensity of Goran Ivanisevic, a favourite of Brian's, calling on God at Wimbledon in times of triumph and in adversity; and another in spotting Brian's links to Firbank and Betjeman. Appropriately, he told mourners that they should look forward to meeting Brian in Heaven, 'where some of us hope to resume our interrupted banquet'.

Dame Ninette de Valois, OM, CH, OBE

1898-2001

Westminster Abbey

THE GATHERING SEASON IS once more upon us. Dame Ninette's memorial must have pride of place this month, but John Warner's was a charming posthumous gesture. The original leading man of *Salad Days* sent his apologies but requested the pleasure of the company of innumerable friends at a party in his memory at the RAC on 11 September. No speeches. Delicious canapés. To emerge to hear of the horrors in New York pinpoints the moment for us.

Two days later Jack Watling (1923-2001) was remembered in that piece, listed as Victor Hugo's, about the ship disappearing over the horizon, which I know as Bishop Brent's *The Ship*. Later, at St Paul's, the pillar of the Royal Theatrical Fund was celebrated by Glyn Kerslake's fresh *I'll See You Again*, his son Giles' fine, funny *About Dad* and Richard Pascoe's resonant *Our Revels Now Are Ended*.

Dame Ninette's commemoration was more intimate than the Abbey's grandest tributes – almost a family service for her extended family of dance stars, fans and trainee *coryphées,* touchingly ranked like great-great-grandchildren. As an overture, Barry Wordsworth and the Royal Ballet Sinfonia treated us to music with which 'Madam' was indelibly associated.

Sir Peter Wright, Director Laureate of the Birmingham Royal Ballet, was a model eulogist, though perhaps the service laid too much emphasis on Dame Ninette's modest writing skills, already illustrated in well-delivered excerpts read by a great-nephew and niece.

Sir Peter was on secure ground detailing her unique creation of a British ballet. He met her in 1943 when he was 17 and she was running the Sadler's Wells company, led by Helpmann and Fonteyn at the New Theatre. She blew in late, full of apologies, a 45-year-old whirlwind, pronounced him 'too old' but conceded that, given two years, 'I might make something of you – if we are still alive.'

None of her stars, supporters and collaborators was forgotten. The original team, Ashton, Lambert, Fedorovitch. The legendary ballerinas. Lilian Bayliss, for whom 'the Lord arranged'. Markova and Dolin, on whom she based her campaign – Dame Alicia was there. Princess Margaret's royal support. Her fondness for working with male dancers – hiring Nureyev 'to stir things up a bit'.

The one time Sir Peter saw her dance (in her fifties) was to celebrate the Company's 25th birthday, reluctantly playing the bossy hostess in *Wedding Bouquet*, magisterially shaking her hips, eyeing the gallery and bringing the house down.

Sir Peter reflected that in her great age Dame Ninette had long wanted to be released. She wondered wrily if God did not want her: but he insisted that God was simply making sure that the ballet could manage without her.

Joan Sims
1930-2001
St Paul's Church, Covent Garden

Sir Harry Secombe, CBE
1921-2001
Westminster Abbey

A FELICITOUS PHRASE IN Dr Wesley Carr's Bidding at the service for Harry Secombe could have done equal duty for Joan Sims. 'Round and rounded' were appropriate words for both cherished entertainers. Both services featured recordings. A *Goon Show* excerpt echoed around the Abbey, ending with awesome BBC footsteps. At St Paul's, Ronnie Cass produced a pirate recording of Joan Sims' sweetly suggestive voice performing *Siren Song*, a timeless number by David Climie and John Pritchett for a station announcer husking out 'When I say Woking...' to the consternation of commuters.

Cass, a genial eulogist and one of the few survivors of the '40s'/'50s' revue, declared that this affection for his subject was evidenced by his 'being prepared to travel on the Northern Line' to get to St Paul's. He recalled her revue break at the old Irving Theatre. Understudying the leading lady, she got laughs where none had been before. The leading lady made an immediate recovery: but the understudy had began her lifelong love affair with the audience.

From her long *Carry On* career he selected one exchange. 'Care to join me in the arbour?' 'I didn't know we were so near the sea.' With the Rev Mark Oakley's express permission, Ronnie Barker and June Whitfield read a correspondence between Barker and Sims laden with *double entendres* on the subject of tits and tit boxes.

THERE WAS PLENTY OF appropriate laughter at the Abbey, too. So many members of the London Welsh Male Choir were on parade that, as they processed through the Quire, I began to think they were on a loop. They gave us a stirring *Men of Harlech* and led their Prince, and us, in *Cwm Rhondda*. Bill Cotton remembered Harry's acknowledgement of any triumph with 'Fooled 'em again!' Michael Parkinson offered the absent Spike Milligan's reflection on 'the sweetness of Wales' and plundered Sir Harry's personal obituary, written in 100 words. 'Records, books, telly, hymns, peritonitis, diabetes, knighthood, *Songs of Praise*, six grandchildren, devoted wife, prostate cancer, stroke, malaria expected soon, winds light to variable.'

Dr Carr had said appropriately that, 'As is so often the case with the clown, the jovial exterior was matched by an inner spirituality.' Jimmy Tarbuck, ascending the high pulpit after the beautiful William Mathias setting of '*Let the people praise Thee, O God*', opened, as Sir Harry might have done, with 'Follow that with the sea lions'. He recalled 'the energy of a pack of hyenas – and the laughs to go with it'; a safari trip on which Sir Harry, 'not speaking bearer', wondered what the delighted bearers had nicknamed him – 'Fat Hippo'.

Finally, he judged that looking down happily on the packed Abbey, Sir Harry's first thought would be, 'Don't let Ken Dodd take the collection!'

Extract from Psalm 67
Let the people praise thee, O God, let all the people praise thee.
Then shall the earth yield her increase; and God,
even our own God, shall bless us.
God shall bless us; and all the ends of the earth shall fear him.

Alan Ross
1922-2001
St Paul's Church, Covent Garden

Larry Adler
1914-2001
Arts Theatre, Great Newport Street

Joseph Cooper, OBE
1912-2001
St Paul's Church, Covent Garden

THE SEA, CRICKET, POETRY and the *London Magazine* were the inevitable themes at Alan Ross' Memorial Service. Jeremy Hutchinson dealt with the sea and Ross' 'Black Dog' days. Harold Pinter and Charles Osborne both claimed prodigious hoards of copies of the magazine. Osborne trumped Pinter with a full set to the playwright's meagre 240. Cricket was a non-starter for Osborne just as opera was for Ross. They soon reached an accommodation. John Woodcock linked Ross with cricket greats Robertson Glasgow, Cardus and Swanton, and conjured up the county ground at Hove in Ross' phrase: 'Sea-scented by the sea.' He also recalled two of Ross' reports for the *Observer*. He wrote of the New Zealand bowler Cunis: 'His bowling was neither fast nor slow. In fact, like his name, it was not quite one thing nor the other.' (Echoing Churchill on the MP Sir Alfred Bossom.) And on the maturing F S Trueman: 'In fast bowling, as in love, control brings better results than youthful enthusiasm.' *Oldie* readers might take a poll.

The young William Boyd was taken to lunch by Ross to celebrate the publication of his first short story. Ross pressed him to a Negroni. He had no idea what a Negroni was but said, in the most sophisticated voice he could manage, 'That would be lovely,' thinking, 'This is the literary life!'

A FEW HOURS LATER a full house at the Arts Theatre remembered Larry Adler and inaugurated his daughter Marmoset's scholarship to the Royal Academy of Music in his name. Larry's Australian protégé, pianist Simon Tedeschi, played two Gershwin preludes, and his younger brother Jerry Adler, a sprightly 83, brought out the mouth organ Larry had encouraged him to play, 'though not as well'. He was fine after a nervous start, which he charmingly dismissed as 'a senior moment'.

IN EULOGISING JOSEPH COOPER, the Lord Armstrong of Ilminster was prodigal rather than economical with the '*actualité*.' Childhood in Westbury on Trym, playing the piano during breaks at his mother's bridge parties, inserting wicked hidden melodies at the expense of some of her guests; scholarship to Clifton, Organ Scholar at Keble, persisting in his interest in jazz and dance music if only to *épater les Académiques*; a pop song, *Sleeping*, for Fay Compton of all people; failing his BMus (Counterpoint) after studying with Armstrong's father at the House; abandoning a piano career which might have led to international success in order to diversify; two happy marriages and then the enduring popularity of *Call the Tune* and *Face the Music*. And so we said Godspeed to three unique *Oldie* contributors. How long, O Lord, how long?

John Walters

1938-2001

BBC Radio Theatre

THE LOVELY ART DECO Radio Theatre is under wraps at the moment while construction or deconstruction goes on around it. However, the pneumatic drills were silenced for an hour to celebrate one of the Corporation's most stimulating and endearing sons.

John Walters produced John Peel's popular Radio One shows, launched the fledgling Andy Kershaw, started the Eddie Grundy fan club, fronted Radio's outstanding oxymoron – a Radio One arts magazine, *Walters' Weekly* – and played for years with a band, The Jazz is Jumping, whose surviving members, now 'potent, grave and reverent signoirs', played us in, played us out and honoured a mutual promise that they would play at each other's obsequies. Walters being the first to go, they steamed through a rousing *Just A Closer Walk With Thee*.

The Rev Ernie Rea, previously Head of Religious Broadcasting, could boast that he had ensnared Walters into compèring a religious programme. Eddie Grundy abandoned his horned hat to become the actor, Trevor Harrison, and introduce Andy Kershaw, whose arrival in the office shared by John Peel and his producer was described by Walters as 'like someone letting a bluebottle out of a jar'. Kershaw identified two personal life-changing events: being ambushed in Rwanda and meeting John Walters. As producer, Walters went home leaving Kershaw to present his first programme live and alone; his judgments were made 'instinctively... a word long absent at the BBC. His philosophy was simple: "We are not here to give the public what it wants. We are here to give it what it does not know it wants."' It was moving, after Kershaw's somewhat ebullient performance, to hear the catch in his voice as he explained that last weekend he felt the urge to ring Walters to enthuse about a boxing fight he had just witnessed – but he could not.

Loudon Wainwright III had mailed a tender country song from Los Angeles – 'There'll be a lot of drinkin' in Heaven/An' eatin' and smokin' and sex.'

Walters discovered Errol Linton busking in the Underground at Oxford Circus. He played two virtuoso solos on the harmonica. Ian Sharp had graduated from sound engineer with Walters to film director. He recalled his subject's interviewing technique – asking a long question and then providing a long answer himself before the interviewee could speak. Waldemar Januszczak backing him up with a memory of the *Venice Biennale* where a moody modern artist responded, 'I'm not having this! This is bollocks!' and left. The recording broadcast the exchange faithfully, topped by Walters' puzzled, 'What happened to him?'

Peter Wylie sang *The Story of the Blues*, Robert Wyatt *September Song* and Chuck Jackson John's favourite song *Any Day Now*. John Peel, who had eulogised John at the funeral, was present as 'J Ravenscroft and family'.

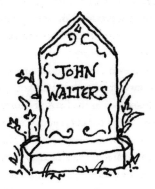

Richard Buckle, CBE

1916-2001

St Paul's Church, Covent Garden

Two simple hymns, *He Who Would True Valour See* and *Lord of the Dance* bookended 'Dickie' Buckle's Memorial Service, to which we were Bidden by the Rev Mark Oakley, who remembered Buckle's weary realisation after one performance that he was 'one Nutcracker nearer death', and how, at an early age, coming upon a portrait of Nijinsky, he found his stare 'a powerful aphrodisiac'. Buckle was a committed advocate and co-founder of the admirable Theatre Museum across the piazza in Covent Garden, still woefully underfunded.

Alexander Schouvaloff read from *The Adventures of a Ballet Critic*, in which the successor to the pioneer critics Haskell, Beaumont and Brahms, skewered those of his colleagues who fell back on 'a fog of definitions' and those whose flattering reviews were designed to secure invitations to dinner. Buckle's principle was 'to know his mind and speak it, even if sometimes he regretted it afterwards'.

Professor Brian Blackwood, who played Chopin's Nocturne Op 32, No2, which balletomanes recognised as the Second Movement of *Les Sylphides*, was Buckle's music researcher on his Nijinsky and Diaghilev books. He started in 1968. Interviewed on a Friday, he was told to start on Monday, 'having read the whole of *A la Recherche du Temps Perdu*'.

A work room was provided. The proximity of the Nag's Head was a comfort. He could drop into rehearsals at Covent Garden. Researching in the British Museum he often shared a desk with Germaine Greer, 'whose thesis subsequently attracted more attention' than his own delving.

Paris, Monte Carlo and Massine's flat in Neuilly became familiar. Buckle took him to tea with Karsavina to seek out the mysteries of *Le Pavillon d'Armide*.

Blackwood picked his way through the score. When he reached the celeste passage he was rewarded by seeing the old prima ballerina leap to her feet and recreate the forgotten steps in her drawing room.

'Dickie', he said, 'knew how far to go too far.'

With a Reminiscence by the critic David Dougill and a Tribute by Julian Barran the great names of ballet fell like the gentle rain from heaven on an appreciative congregation: Dolin and Diaghilev, Rambert, and Romola Nijinsky, Sokolova, Idzikowski, Woizikowski, Buckle's brilliant ballet exhibitions and gala dance evenings. His flat, in the heart of Covent Garden, in Henrietta Street. His unconventional greetings – 'Hallo, you hairy pig.' His idea of making an exhibition of 'Dickie Buckle's flat – Just As It Is'. His collection of shoes. 'Have you seen Dickie Buckle's latest shoes?' Someone asked Jerome Robbins. 'I certainly hope so.'

Barran emphasised Buckle's generosity and encouragement to the young in the art world; recalled a gaffe, mistaking Buckle for the corpulent Douglas Cooper, 'which pleased neither of them'; and described in a memorable vignette his discovery of a Caravaggio found above the bed of an admiral's bedroom: 'first viewed from a very unusual angle'.

Lord of the Dance *(Sydney Carter)*
Dance, then, wherever you may be;
I am the Lord of the Dance, said he,
And I'll lead you all, wherever you may be,
And I'll lead you all in the dance, said he.

HRH The Princess Margaret, Countess of Snowdon

1930-2002

Westminster Abbey

THE ROYAL FAMILY TURNED out in force for this service of Thanksgiving. The mood, serious but celebratory, accommodated the Abbey's accustomed grandeur. Its choir, joined by King's Cambridge and St George's Chapel Windsor, was backed up by the Academy of St Martin's-in-the-Fields and Andrew Reid at the organ.

Princess Margaret wished the service be set around Fauré's *Requiem*, Dame Felicity Lott sang *Pie Jesu* and Bryn Terfel *Libera Me*. Viscount Linley read from *I Corinthians* 15: '... this mortal must put on immortality', and a member of the extended family, Felicity Kendal (her agent is Lady Sarah Chatto's mother-in-law), read *The Union of Friends* from William Penn's *Some Fruits of Solitude*: 'They that love beyond the world cannot be separated by it...' It came up a great deal fresher than popping into poor Henry Holland's 'next room'.

The Princess rejected a eulogy – usually my text. The Dean suggested we recall our own memories of her – mine all happy. First meeting her in 1963 with David Frost at a party. 'Why don't you "satirise" the reverential way the BBC report us?' she asked. Frost remembered Ian Lang's Footlights monologue, 'The Sinking of the Queen's Barge', which shocked the nation the next week.

Years later, taking her home from a Laine/Dankworth evening at Ronnie Scott's. Along the Fulham Road we passed a boarded-up shop. 'They used to sell clothes in there. They called it "The Countess of Snowdon". People thought I was selling off my old dresses.' Rashly, I suggested: 'It must be difficult for you, Ma'am. You've got that restaurant at the back o... called "Maggie Jones". 'Ned! I *am* the Countess of Snowdon. I hav... been called Maggie Jones.'

Off to Los Angeles. Which hotel? In the last one the beds had been uncomfortable. She and her lady-in-waiting piled the sofa cushions high on the mattress. 'I felt like the Princess and the Pea.'

At the Ivy, deftly sidestepping an egregious night-club owner determined to hobnob. At Lacy's after *The Mitford Girls*, bringing joy to Margaret Costa, whose husband was cooking. At Sadler's Wells at a very early AIDS charity performance of an 18th-century, doggerel, burlesque version of Hamlet, shouting to me, 'My God, it's Vera!' as Vera Lynn picked her way through the bodies at the end singing 'We'll Meet Again'. Greeting Maurice Denham (First Gravedigger) with 'Oh! It's the lift man!' (In the '30s, Maurice installed the lifts at 145 Piccadilly and gave the little Princesses rides up and down.)

Good idea to cut the eulogies. In future your critic will measure his memories against them.

...MPECCABLE eulogists to recall all 'Brommers'' Greatest Hits. ...ge had the advantage of going first, having known him since 7 Sep... mber 1957, when both were junior reporters covering a Third Division football game – they set a pattern by quickly adjourning for a gin and tonic.

Bromley was to move from the *Dagenham Post* via the doomed *Daily Herald* to the *Daily Mirror*, before landing up at early commercial television as a novice sports producer, soon faced with the challenge of the BBC's *Grandstand*. He hoped to pinch the American title, *Wide World of Sport*, but with table tennis at Wembley, snooker at the National Liberal Club, wrestling from Shoreditch and racing from Sandown he quickly dropped 'Wide' and settled for *World of Sport*.

It fell to Wooldridge to tell the notorious 'Rififi' story. In a court battle with an American fight promoter the boxing man's QC asked Bromley 'If it was his custom to draw up a contract of this complexity on the napkin of a night club called [pause for maximum effect] the Rififi?' After some consideration Bromley smiled broadly and answered, 'Certainly.' In the last days of his illness a sign on the door of his hospital room read, 'The Rififi Club'.

When Wooldridge rang Richie Benaud in Australia to break the news of his death, Benaud said, 'I shan't mourn him. I shall simply drink a toast to the long friendship we've all had with a wonderful man.' It reminded Wooldridge of an obituary by Red Smith, the late sports columnist of the *New York Times*: 'Death is no big deal. The least of us can accomplish that. Living is the trick.'

Geoffrey Clever, a long-time colleague, grabbed Brommers' favourite joke. I'll try to condense it in Jingle-speak: 'Inn sign – advertises A Pint,

A Pie, A Friendly Word – Customer buys Pint and Pie – asks Landlord – "Friendly Word?" – Landlord – "Don't eat Pie!'"

Michael Grade started work as Bromley's gofer at the *Mirror*. He speculated on his old boss' attitude to the service: 'Get 'em on to the G and Ts. This is a party, not a bloody funeral – oh, and charge it to *World of Sport*.' He recalled their 'Snatch of the Day' battle with the BBC over football; an office outing to Bloom's – 'Quick bacon and eggs, mate?' – and concluded, fighting to control his emotions and just succeeding, 'He taught me all I know about journalism. Unfortunately, not all *he* knew.'

Poor Jimmy Tarbuck had to follow three fine, loudly applauded eulogies, and did so in style. 'He was modest about his golf. He was entitled to be.' At the end of one game Brommers asked, 'What shall I give the caddy?' 'Your clubs.' 'If he'd been organising this we'd have been in Langan's half an hour ago.'

We were read to by Peter Saunders, Rachael Heyhoe Flint and Neil Durden-Smith; welcomed and blessed by the Rev Liz Russell; and led in prayer by the Rev Roger Royle, who reckoned that the lusty singing of *Praise My Soul The King of Heaven* put *Songs of Praise* to shame.

Irene Worth
1916-2002
Almeida, King's Cross

Barbara Ethel Newman
1914-2002
St Paul's Church, Covent Garden

TWO ARTISTS, BOTH ALIKE in dignity – but not much else. Irene Worth, a great tragedienne, was celebrated by a full house at the peripatetic Almeida. Barbara Newman, the definitive Goose in pantomime, rallied a devoted 30-odd at St Paul's. Both were held in similar affection.

At King's Cross popular actors paid homage to Irene's great roles. Zoe Wanamaker, Toby Stephens, Eileen Atkins, Penelope Wilton, Janet Suzman, Anna Massey, and Ian MacDiarmid alternated with music from the Menuhin School Quartet and Ronald McGill.

Peter Eyre, her devoted colleague in later years ('Being a friend of Irene meant a lot of driving') introduced two moving recordings. David Hare evoked her fierce intelligence – not the famous impression of one performer: 'Acting with Irene was like being a speck on the carpet and seeing a huge Hoover coming towards you.'

Hare was disconcerted when she habitually called him 'Teach', but remembered vividly that he had 'once learnt the limits of Irene's self criticism'; and that telling her he'd heard that Coral Browne was good as Gertrude provoked her to say, 'I find that very hard to believe.'

Which reminds me of Coral on Irene: 'Of course, she's a negress, I've dressed with her. Seen her nipples.'

Barbara Newman was two years older then Irene, a *pierrot*, a concert party *soubrette*, and finally Priscilla, the Goose. The great Principal Boy, Dorothy

Ward, hated *Mother Goose*. Her role was Colin. 'No acting to get your teeth into – not like Jack or Dick.' But Ms Newman made Priscilla her own.

Her eccentricities were described by Jack Seaton of BMHS as 'character', and by the principal eulogist, John Inman, as 'stark, raving bonkers'.

Inman played *Mother Goose* with her 14 times. First at Wimbledon in 1976. She reminded him of a tiny Margaret Rutherford in cape and hat. They met in a recently repainted white rehearsal room. Arthur English, playing the Squire, pointed to the white-flecked floor. 'Ya see,' he kicked at the blanched spots. 'These animal acts don't take long to get into character.'

When they ran the lines for the first time, Inman made the mistake of looking down to her face. 'It's no good looking down there,' she snapped, indicating the height of her costume head, 'I'll be up in here!'

One Christmas in Bristol, Inman treated her to a light new wicker goose frame, lovingly woven by the local Blind School. She stored it on the bed in her tiny flat, lowering it to the floor when she slept. She was surrounded by 'geese' sent by fans. Goose cushions, fluffy geese, goose lampshades. In one of her favourite words, 'Geese galore!'

She also insisted on the 18th-century offer of 'A dish of tea?' I hope she rhymed it along with Pope: 'Here thou, great Anna! Whom three realms obey,/Dost sometimes counsel take – and sometimes tea.'

Dame Dorothy Tutin

1930-2001

St Paul's Church, Covent Garden

Spike Milligan, KBE

1915-2002

St Martin-in-the-Fields

PLAYING THAT GAME OF degrees of separation, I can unite Dame Dorothy and (Sir) Spike in one move. Dottie was Cicely to Joan Greenwood's Gwendolen in *The Importance* (1959). Joan was Spike's leading lady (a bumpier ride) in *Oblomov* (1964).

Mark Oakley is stepping up his homework. For the *Bidding* he researched Tynan on Tutin, 'ablaze like a diamond in a mine'; leaving Patrick Garland to recall another of Ken's shafts, her voice 'cooing like a turtle dove with laryngitis'. Garland's own memory was, 'I left no ring for her...' in Peter Hall's autumnal *Twelfth Night*. Her magic? 'It is too hard a knot for me t'untie.'

Corin Redgrave, standing in to read Keith Baxter's tribute, had experienced his own infatuation, waiting for hours on Cheyne Walk staring at her houseboat. Baxter was bewitched from the time he saw her from the balcony at the Phoenix outshining a starry cast as Hero in *Much Ado*. In his mind's eye he saw her always dancing – nearly to the end at her son's wedding.

Virginia McKenna reported Dorothy's wish to return as a butterfly ghost and remarked upon the appearance of one Red Admiral at her Chichester funeral and another during the interval of a Waring family concert. Her reading, Arthur Waley's *Three Ways of Ancient China*, and Nick Waring's, *The Ascent of Everest* by Sir John Hunt (acknowledging his mother's love of mountains and her adventurous spirit), were refreshingly original.

Amanda Waring spoke with ringing pride of her mother's brave 'scenarios for the future – generally wrong'. Canon John Hester shyly produced a faded photograph Dottie sent him in reply to his fan letter when, as a curate, his bishop took him to see *The Living Room* in 1953.

SPIKE'S FUNNY, MOVING SEND-OFF has been widely reported. Stephen Fry introduced Matthew, Chapter 11: 'If you can make head or tail of it, you have my undying respect.' He finished, 'This is the word of the Lord,' adding: '"Are you Jewish?" "No, a tree fell on me." This is the word of Spike.'

Barbara Dickson sang Spike's favourite song, *Here's That Rainy Day*. Peter O'Toole spoke Sonnet 30, 'All losses are restored and sorrows end', saying, 'Spike liked the sonnets better: "They're short," he said.' Jane Milligan sang *Alice* – Spike's words, Alan Clare's music. David Secombe trumped Spike's wish to die after Harry Secombe so that Harry couldn't sing *Guide Me, O Thou Great Redeemer* for him by producing a recording.

Eric Sykes was the only possible eulogist. He remembered Spike, en route to lunch in Shepherd's Bush, lying on the pavement outside an undertaker's shouting, 'Shop!' 'It only took them 50 years to answer!'

Barry Took

1928-2002

St John's Wood Church

THERE WAS ONCE AN actor whose entry in *Spotlight* read: 'Charles (formerly Percy)...' There were 30-odd 'formerly's at the packed church for Barry Took – 'formerly' producers, chief press officers, managing directors, chairmen, heads of LE, editors, executive producers, BBC secretaries, *Radio Times* photographers – all celebrating an inspirational career.

Geoffrey Durham found the perfect word for Barry's occasional cussedness – 'curmudgeonly'. Not since Douglas Bunn used 'skinflint' at Harry Llewellyn's farewell have I heard a word of criticism so precisely chosen.

Durham defined Took's laugh as 'H double EE as spelt', and his pride in *Round the Horne* and the joke which spawned its longest laugh: they named the head of the Football Association 'Sweet' so that he could answer the phone, 'Sweet, FA.' (Echoes of the company which the late David Land called 'Hope and Glory' for similar reasons.)

Michael McLain explained Hugh Carleton Greene's acceptance of Barry's *double-entendres*: 'I like dirty scripts.' Margaret Thatcher thought it 'so clever to be able to think of funny things' and wanted some gags. Took warned that one of his *Laugh-In* jokes turned up on Nixon's lips. 'And look what happened to him,' said Mrs T.

Dilly Keane played '*Ritz*', the only song she and Barry completed for a 'chamber musical' ('with scenes in Versailles, Baden-Baden and the kitchens of the Carlton Hotel'). Barry reckoned 'snappy songs should cheer up this dreary synopsis'. The congregation produced an effective tap routine sound by banging coins on the backs of pews.

Perhaps Barry Took's permanent achievement was to midwife the birth of *Barry Took's Flying Circus,* subsequently *Monty Python's*. The late Michael Mills ('formerly' Head of LE) whimsically called the Pythons 'your children by Greer Garson'.

Terry Jones gratefully sketched the genesis of the Pythons. John Cleese, pretending that this was *his* brief, then addressed himself to the rest of Barry's career, starting as a Caroll Levis discovery. Murmurs of recognition at Levis' name prompted him to cry, 'Hello, old people!' Towards the end of Took's career, 'Like many of us, when we are too old or too stupid to write, he turned into a performer.'

Alan Coren used to picnic with Barry in the churchyard of St John's – 'between Lord's and the Lord'. Barry always ordered 'two rounds of salt beef, and make it lean', simply so that he could hear Sam, the delicatessen assistant, say, 'Lean? Which way?' In the churchyard they 'laughed until the crumbs flew', especially at the decaying look of the MCC members across the road. Took advanced the conceit that they must have been taken in by the Distressed Gentlefolks Association and 'distressed' to perfect their decrepit appearance.

James Moir, Michael Palin and one of Barry's children, Eleanor, added postscripts to the Order of Service, more memories to add to *Round the Horne*, *Beyond Our Ken*, *The Army Game*, *Bootsy and Snudge*, *Python* and the literacy programmes of which Barry was probably most proud. Not a bad score.

Sir Peter Parker, KBE, LVO

1924-2002

St Martin-in-the-Fields

THE AUTHOR OF *Mrs Miniver*, Jan Struther, is leaping up the Memorial Hit Parade with *Lord of all Hopefulness*. Sir Peter's service was one of three to programme it in a very few weeks. A queue of eulogists honoured Sir Peter and his many achievements. Rayne Kruger quoted, 'The evil that men do lives after them.' Not only was there no evil in his old friend, but, 'with his Blakeian mystical sense of the Divine', he saw none in others.

David Howell emphasised Sir Peter's Japanese connections through Mitsubishi. His part in the 1991 Japanese Festival did more for Anglo-Japanese understanding than the recent World Cup. 'He was fascinated by the subtlety and, dare I say, ambiguity of his Japanese colleagues, embracing a management style 99 per cent the same but different in all important respects!'

Bert Gemmell recalled 'the Railway Years' (1977-1983): 'Inspired management, chairmanship, leadership... he made us feel like a family again.' Asked what he was doing in Scotland, Sir Peter replied that he was on a 'Thistle-stop tour'. On another journey there was a death on the track. The guard, encouraged to explain the delay, offered, 'The Chairman is on board and there has been a fertility on the line.'

Peter's sons, Nathaniel and Oliver, spoke two pieces of William Blake, an inspiration throughout their father's life. The slow movement of Bach's Concerto for two violins in D minor, *largo ma non tanto*, preceded Lucy, Peter's daughter, who read *Sunlight On The Garden* by Louis MacNeice, another favourite of her father's, and introduced two scene-stealing grandchildren.

Richard Eyre, with the unenviable task of following them, handled his subject's theatricality, his support of the National Theatre, the Young Vic and Shakespeare's Globe and his 'two Lears before he was 25'. 'In spite of everything he missed his vocation... he was an actor... larger than life... Or life, perhaps, was smaller than Peter.'

Professor Anthony Giddens, director of the LSE, testified that, as Chairman of the Governors, he 'understood the nature of academic life, not a common trait of businessmen'. Alan, the oldest of the Parker boys, all so alike and so like their father, brought us back to his parents' unparalleled devotion to one another – a suitable cue for the Beatitudes.

John Thaw
1942-2002
St Martin-in-the-Fields
Dr Patrick Woodcock
1920-2002
St John's, Smith Square

I CONFESS TO GATECRASHING John Thaw's service, having only heard about it two days earlier. The Medici String Quartet featured special arrangements by Morse's Barrington Phelong, including a rousing setting of *The Sun Has Got His Hat On*.

Tom Courtenay, who weaned John from Cannonball Adderley and on to Schubert's B Flat Trio, also converted him from 'a suspicious manner which did not invite conversation' to a close friendship where they could slip into 'a game of talking as though we had no teeth', in which they persisted. 'I don't know why we did it; but we did it a lot and John was very good at it.'

Richard Briers, like Thaw 'a world-class whinger', evoked his host's reluctance to take advice when ruining sausages on a barbecue. 'He didn't like notes.'

Abigail Thaw's moving, simple poem was prompted by the family's gift of a 60th birthday visit to Barcelona which was defeated by her father's death. 'Last week we went to Barcelona/He really should have come/We missed him...'

Kevin Whately spoke of the fun this remarkable actor inspired on set. 'I can't say this rubbish! I am a Commander of the British Empire!' To an over-ebullient director yelling 'Cut!' 'What did he call me?' And, imitating schedulers planning future programmes, '...that little, fat, white-haired one ...that John Thaw'.

Richard Attenborough remarked on Thaw's own scholarship to the RADA and his confidential generosity in funding bursaries so that others might have the same chance.

As we left St Martin's, 60 'ecologically friendly' balloons inscribed 'Today we remembered John with love' sailed skywards.

AT ST JOHN'S, IN IDIOSYNCRATIC English, Estelle Welldon hosted a celebration of Patrick Woodcock, glorious doctor to the theatre. He sent her to a speech therapist who returned her saying her accent was destroying his. David Hughes recalled, 'the warm asperity of his bedside manner… inside this incisive curmudgeon was a romantic striving not to get out.'

Sheila Gish recited the names of her least favourite directors while he punctured her bottom with a B12 shot. Judy Campbell fractured hip, arm and ankle on the ancient cobbles of Nîmes and forbore to scream in hospital lest Patrick be ashamed. She was, after all, British.

Alec McCowen ('How's the play? Leading lady? Director?' 'Patrick, I'm in pain!' 'Sorry, I forgot') added a virtuoso spoken 'You're The Top!' Touching memories came from Patrick's French housekeeper. Chita Riviera first fell for Dr Woodcock's name, 'with all its American *double-entendres*'.

A barn-storming Alan Bates shook St John's with an outrageously accurate and affectionate impersonation. John Williams played Bach and Mangore. Finally Daniel Welldon read Patrick's own words: 'A meeting between two oldies invariably degenerates into an organ recital.'

Bryan Pringle
1935-2002
Gerald Theron Campion
1921-2002

Both at St Paul's Church, Covent Garden

TWO SERVICES WITHIN A month of each other produced a rush of affectionate rib-tickling reminiscences – in Pringle's case I'll list the eulogists; you can split the stories between them. Tim Wylton, Nicholas Geeks, Alison Steadman, Graham Benson and Alan Plater spoke.

Musical memories included *My Fair Lady*, *Billy*, *The Boyfriend* and Alan Plater's *Coal House Door* show, admirably played by Kenny Clayton, who is not the famous pianist who performed at one service, sank his sorrows too enthusiastically at the wake and threw up into the piano, mournfully pleading, 'It's what he would have wanted.'

We had Pringle 'the sweater'; Pringle 'the son of a vicar – not always a good start in life'; Pringle on Pringle: 'I was born with a face nobody could think well of'; Pringle drunk in charge of a tandem going alone the wrong way up a one-way street: 'I'm looking for my passenger, officer'; Pringle's explanations for many castings: 'Bernard Cribbins Not Available'; Pringle's favourite story: Two old actors discuss a provincial tour: 'Not much of a play. Not much of a part. But there's a cake in the second act!' And we had Brian Patten's *How Long is a Man's Life?*, Robertson-Glasgow on cricket and 'What is the matter with Radio Four...'. 'We miss Bryan Pringle. That is the matter with Radio Four.'

Two rules had to be observed in Gerry Campion's Soho club ('the one under the ladies' knickers shop'): 1) Leave your credits at the door; 2) Don't mention the Fat Boy. (Gerry was the TV Billy Bunter. Interviewed once at Broadcasting

House, he was asked for 'a few "yaroos" to round it off'. He was ha
balk for £10, but, 'if you want a performance, "yaroos" are £50 each!')

John Junkin remembered him throwing out Lee Marvin, his generosity
and his rule of only insulting people he liked. Brian Peck revealed that on
Gerry's mother's side he shared grandparents with Charlie Chaplin.

Keith Waterhouse declared that if there had been no word for 'irascible'
it would have been necessary to invent it for Campion; recalled a cream-pie
incident which left the innocent victim barred, and the incident which gave
him a setting for Jeffrey Bernard's reminiscences. John Murphy, Granada's
casting director, fell asleep on the lavatory at Gerry's and was locked in for the
night. A conspicuous drinker, he rang the landlord at home in St John's Wood.
Fearing for his vodka stocks, Gerry made it to the club in three minutes.

We heard of food which Gerry cooked, of the Buckstone and of France,
which he loved. Jazz classics threaded the contributions – others from Angelica
Campion and Brian Rix. *Ain't Misbehavin'*, *Stars Fell on Alabama*, *I Feel So
High* and *Georgia on my Mind* were a poignant counterpoint to the hilarity.

an Tagg

1928-2002

ul's Church, Covent Garden

beth, Countess
of Longford

1906-2002

Memorial Mass, Westminster Cathedral

WHAT A WEALTH OF admiring and affectionate reminiscence the stage designer Alan Tagg's Memorial Service inspired. Mark Oakley recalled Olivier's description, 'that kitten with steel claws'. Joan, Lady Olivier, concurred: 'After hours of wrangling, quietly, politely, Alan got his own way.' Michael Halifax, exuded bonhomie. They met in 1956. Tagg presented a modest set for *Look Back in Anger*. The fledgling Royal Court had a rule: no money for scenery. Halifax was overruled. There had to be a window. Something must surround it. At Peter Jones, Tagg looked at material. Bolt after bolt was cooed over and rejected. Finally, the exhausted shop boy left to get a piece he had spied in a store-room corner. He never returned. *A Member of the Wedding* had the designer in a Deep South, 'Spanish moss' mode, pleading, 'Just another dab of Spanish moss.' Four plays later, for *The Long and the Short and the Tall* he was in 'Jungle' mode: 'Just one more large leaf, *please*.'

Joanna David read Christina Rossetti's *When I Am Dead, My Dearest*. Tagg had admired it at Ingrid Bergman's Memorial Service. Closest to Alan Tagg, Charles Colville detailed his qualified reluctance to communicate with neighbours in the Languedoc: 'But when 'e *want* something M. Tagg speak French.' Edward Fox once witnessed the designer filling abandoned footballs in his mother's garden with concrete and painting them pink. 'His soul is with God. His balls are in Sussex.'

Oldie readers should be proud of our Wireless critic who – an early candidate for the Catherine Pakenham Award for young journalists – impeccably eulogised Elizabeth Longford. She had to follow the Homily of the Cardinal Archbishop of Westminster, who finished strongly with Proverbs 31, verse 28: 'Strength and honour are her clothing and she shall rejoice in time to come... many daughters have done virtuously, but thou excellest them all.' Verse 27 is particularly apposite too: 'She eateth not the bread of idleness.' Valerie Grove's strongest sallies in recalling Elizabeth Longford's 'incomparable matriarchy' pinpointed her job as a Beaverbrook columnist, 'A Mother With Something to Say'; and Evelyn Waugh's reaction to *The Pakenham Party Book*: 'Laura has never given a party in her life. Pray God this book does not inspire her to do so.'

Antonia Pinter wisely brought her own Song of Solomon for 'Rise up, my love, my fair one', sparing us the printed, 'Come then, my love'. Her poor brother Michael was lumbered with the Cathedral's Corinthians 13 and 'Love' – no substitute for 'Charity'.

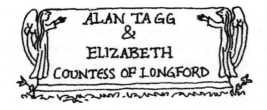

When I Am Dead, My Dearest *(Christina Rossetti)*
When I am dead, my dearest,
Sing no sad songs for me;
Plant thou no roses at my head,
Nor shady cypress tree:
Be the green grass above me
With showers and dewdrops wet;
And if thou wilt, remember,
And if thou wilt, forget.

Anthony John Elwyn Besch

1924-2002

St Paul's Church, Covent Garden

CAROLINE BOWERS ORGANISED HER uncle's Memorial. What a good job she did! From his insistence on 'blue and white flowers only' to her memory of 'Anton' near death. An old lady in a nearby bed launched into a folk tune. His visitor said sympathetically, 'What a lovely song!' Anthony, the perfectionist, barked out, 'Completely out of tune from start to finish.'

St Paul's enjoyed an appropriately operatic occasion. As the Rev Mark Oakley whispered, 'There's no business like holy show business', before his 'welcome' inspired by John Donne's 'one equal music' sermon. Among the musical Great and Good were Sirs Colin Davis and Charles Mackerras, Robert Ponsonby and Thomas Hemsley.

Students from the Britten School at the Royal College and from the Guildhall sang excerpts from *Così fan tutte*, *Der Rosenkavalier* and *Albert Herring*. Lady Billows should look like Baroness Trumpington, who was also in the church. The clever soprano, Claire Surman, could pass for Lady T's granddaughter, but the authority was there. Christopher Bass read from his uncle's early memoir: the model theatre, father-built, complete with fly tower; school play appearance as Anna, mother of Tobias in Bridie's *Tobias and the Angel*; and, at Oxford, speaking the prophetic line, 'Whoever gets a taste for the theatre will never get rid of it', in Goldoni's *The Impresario*.

In 1944, on an army exercise, he struggled through Sussex grass. Topping a steep rise, he consulted his Ordnance Survey map. Looking down, he identified – Glyndebourne! Soon Sir George Christie was there with him – 'assistant to Anthony Besch' who was 'assistant to Carl Ebert'. From Sir George's affectionate but indistinct eulogy, I only gleaned odd words – Stravinsky, Rake's Progress, Bath Festival, Oliver Messel, Tommy Beecham,

La Clemenza di Tito, scholarship, 'an intellectual aristocrat with a neat wit'. We got the message.

No trouble hearing Timothy West's *Death be not proud* or his Oxford Betjeman, or Michael Godley's 'a new heaven and a new earth', or the story of John Pritchard abandoning his baton to Basil while he checked acoustics at the back of Glyndebourne stalls. Anthony entered crying, 'What is Basil doing queering John's pitch?'

Dame Janet Baker proudly confessed to starting her career in 1957 in the Glyndebourne chorus – and to learning how to work from Anthony Besch – lessons in stamina and dedication. Barry Humphries remembered, but did not disclose, the secret ingredient in Anthony's mango ice-cream. Thetis Blacker memorably recited a sonnet which he wrote in 1955 on Chelsea Embankment when he arrived for tea with her in Danvers Street. She had forgotten and was from home.

His last visit to the theatre was *Dick Whittington* at Windsor. Some 50 years before, he had started his professional career there as a deck hand in the same pantomime.

Irving Nicholas Davies

1926-2002

St Paul's Church, Covent Garden

ANTHONY BURGESS ONCE REVIEWED his own novel under a pseudonym. I'd better come clean. I organised Irving Davies' Memorial Service. It might, I thought, be interesting to examine the effect of 'Lo! these many years' of Memorial reviewing for *The Oldie*.

The hymn *Come to us Creative Spirit*, ideal for a leading dancer/choreographer, I heard at Leslie Edwards' celebration. 'Craftsman actor, graceful dancer' hits the button. Sung to a rousing E G Monk tune, it takes off after Mark Oakley's always thoughtful Bidding.

David Suchet – no dancer – praised Irving's ability to transform him and a host of other stars into movers – him as Sid Field, all of them as guests in *The Play What I Wrote*. David read Sonnet 30 beautifully: 'But if the while I think of thee, dear friend,/All losses are restored and sorrows end.' A trawl through the Sonnets always pays off.

I 'discovered' the choir of St Bride's at the cartoonist Jak's send-off. They sang a stirring anthem, *Bring Us O Lord God*, a fierce descant on *Lord of the Dance* and their speciality, a magical medley of show songs featuring especially 'Who Do You Love, I Hope?' and 'Why Can't You Behave?', Irving's numbers in *Annie Get Your Gun* (1947) and *Kiss Me Kate* for the opening of BBC 2 (1964).

In helping us understand his firm belief in the Maharishi's Transcendental Meditation, David Morgan was simple and witty. He added a vivid vignette of the dancer in an exquisite pale Armani suit, quizzed by a stuffy businessman. 'What are you in?' 'Shipping,' Irving said, not missing a beat. (And he did choreograph cruise cabarets.)

There were four collaborators on the show Bertie: Anita Harris, Mike Margolis, the composer Kenny Clayton and Irving. His remark, 'It's our show,' inspired Ms Harris' show-biz anthem.

Wendy Toye auditioned 16-year-old Irving in 1943. They were friends for 60 years – so, Cicero on Friendship, which I heard at John Higgins' service.

Irving was in shows by Noël Coward and Joyce Grenfell. I gave Cilla Black two memorial favourites – *I'm Here for a Short Visit Only*, by Coward, and Grenfell's *If I Should Go Before The Rest Of You*. Cilla added wicked 40-year-old memories of Irving weaning her from her native 'Scouse'. He introduced her to the mysterious gipsy dancers' language, 'Polare' and 'Vada the bona polone'.

Twenty minutes is a long time for a eulogy, but Irving's 76 years and his crowded, distinguished career demanded no less. He had danced for Gene Kelly, choreographed Sokolova, Hinton Battle, Ann Reinking and three generations of leading British showbiz dancers; coaxed and inspired countless leading ladies and clumsy actors to believe that they moved gracefully; all with an abiding energy, artistry and sweetness – always offering his favourite encouragement, 'Super, darlings, it worked.'

Simon Gutteridge played us out with *We Bring You Sunshine* (always try for a smile up the aisle); but the congregation, including many of Irving's seasoned dancers over the years, lingered long, a reunion cocktail party, blissfully unaware of the absence of drink.

'Paddy' Maloney

1916-2003

St Bride's Church, Fleet Street

Lord Wilberforce, CMG, OBE

1907-2003

St Margaret's, Westminster

Maurice Denham, OBE

1909-2002

St Paul's Church, Covent Garden

Debbie Barham

1976-2003

St Paul's Church, Covent Garden

CANON JOHN OATES RETURNED to St Bride's to join David Meara in celebrating 'Paddy' Maloney's long life. Paddy's son, Mark, sketched the highs and lows of a switchback career in exhibition organising. Before the St Bride's Choir's inspiring Easter Hymn from *Cavalleria Rusticana*, Neil Benson affectionately remembered Paddy's devotion to the Saints and Sinners Club, and an endearing trait. He would say, 'I knew your father,' to any member. If Paddy met Jesus in Heaven, his first words would be, 'I know your Father.'

LORD WILBERFORCE'S CAREER AS a revered judge was addressed by Lord Neill of Bladon and Professor Cecil Olmstead after the Lord Chancellor had socially worked the pews up front. The denazification of Germany, 465 appeals, and the anti-slavery tradition of the family came into focus. Neil recognised Wilberforce's impeccable conduct but found him 'deadliest when sitting silent and unconvinced'. The professor had a good phrase: 'He burnished the lineage of a fine family.' So did his grandson, Richard, who with a chorister, Stephen Douse, led the choir beautifully in *O Death, Where Is Thy Sting*?

AFFECTION FLOWED FROM CONGREGATION and eulogists at Maurice Denham's farewell. So busy was Maurice with the wireless in the '40s and '50s that one producer's daughter thought his full name was 'And Maurice Denham of course'. In his last years at Denville Hall he was the ladies' adored favourite, though Julian Glover recalled a recent jealous actory stirring when Maurice announced that he had, at his age, 'got another job'. From *Much Binding in the Marsh* to *Talking to a Stranger* he was superb, as Linda Marlow, Jane Lapotaire, Dickie Attenborough and Tim Denham confirmed.

AT 16, DEBBIE BARHAM became a professional gag writer, extravagantly prolific and daringly funny. She supplied innumerable comics until her death at 26. Her father's insistence that Bruce Hyman, John McVicar and John Langdon lace the occasion with her jokes helped lift the sadness. Clive Anderson reckoned it was the first C of E service to quote texts from the Koran and Victor Lewis Smith. Readings from Debbie's emails produced gales of laughter.

'Paddy' Maloney
Lord Wilberforce
Maurice Denham
Debbie Barham

Sir Hardy Amies, KCVO

1909-2003

St James's Church, Piccadilly

SIR HARDY WROTE MOST of this review himself. He also supplied a silk
Hardy Amies bookmark for the Order of Service, which was decorated with
the legend '*Impar arte, negotio superior*', 'Less than art, more than trade'.

Readings were cunningly chosen. Mrs J Enoch Powell, widow of Hardy's
old army companion, was given Exodus 28.3, 'You shall make sacred
vestments for the glorious adornment of your brother Aaron'. I would like
to quote it all. Make do with: 'They shall make an ephod of gold, of blue,
purple and crimson yarns, and of fine twisted linen, skilfully worked'. And,
if you're wondering, an ephod is 'a sleeveless garment worn by priests in
ancient Israel'.

The Order of Service was studded with Sir Hardy's aphorisms. 'The
desire for new clothes is as old as Adam and Eve and the fig-leaf.' 'The urge
to make love is perhaps the biggest incentive to dress well.' 'The suit is the
livery for living.'

'A man should look as if he had bought his clothes with intelligence, put
them on with care and then forgotten all about them.' 'I expect to see God
in a five-button suit.'

Derek Granger read Sir Hardy's piece about his country home and the
four Acts of his garden – snowdrops, tulips, roses, *Nicotiana sylvestris*.

The Duchess of Devonshire (best-dressed woman there by a country
mile) read from his *Oldie* interview with Naim Attallah. She betrayed
herself with something between a grimace and a giggle when she came to:
'My favourite duchess gave a very important private ball for which she wore
a 25-year-old dress. She had a new dress made by me for a staff ball which
took place the day before so that the staff could not say that Her Grace was

wearing an old dress. But for her own proper ball she wore an old dress and she looked marvellous. That is English style at its best.'

On his Royal Victorian Order: 'I don't think she ever intended it for dressmakers.' 'Have you ever fallen madly in love?' 'Oh yes, every week, mostly with the milkman.'

More revelations came in Selina Hastings's affectioniate address. 'Kim Philby was always pumping me for information.' 'Good God, what about?' 'My tailor, of course.' A dubious stately home was recalled, and 'the chink of the footmen's bracelets as they recovered the plates at dinner'. And Buddy Roger's alarm when caught wearing ruby cufflinks: 'Don't tell Hardy. He'll say they're ageing.'

Best of all, the last day of his distinguished Army career. He reported to be congratulated by his commanding officer. He had designed the uniform himself. 'Those buttons, Amies, are they regulation?' 'No, sir, a pansy resting on his laurels.'

Elisabeth Welch

1904-2003

The Chapel, Breakspeare Crematorium

IF THE ANTI-MEMORIAL Service movement continues, some (well, one) of us will be out of a job. Robert Morley didn't want one. Nor did John Gielgud or Alec Guinness. Elisabeth Welch was of the same mind. Dying this year, seven months short of her 100th birthday, she is certainly *Oldie* material.

The Rev Ian Wiseman had done his homework and brought a warm intimacy to the clinical chapel. So did vintage Welch recordings. Moyra Fraser read three pieces of Shakespeare, chosen by Derek Granger, featuring music – 'If music be the food of love...', 'Orpheus with his lute...' and 'The isle is full of noises, sounds and sweet airs'. Granger then quoted generous obituaries and reminded us of Frank Rich's '80s' *New York Times* plea that Lis be declared a 'National Treasure' and never again allowed to leave her native America. She had returned in triumph some 50 years after her first big Broadway success when, at Irving Berlin's suggestion, she rescued Cole Porter's *Love For Sale*, sinking in his show *The New Yorkers*.

I am indebted to the eulogist for his notes in which he attempted to cram 100 years into 10 minutes. Her father was half Native-American, half African-American, her mother part Irish, part Scots. She grew up where the Lincoln Center now stands. In the '20s she appeared in *Running Wild* and *Blackbirds*. Shocked, her father disappeared from her life. 'Girlie's gone on the boards,' he lamented. 'She's lost!'

From Paris she attacked London in Porter's *Nymph Errant* with her trademark 'Solomon'. Agate's critique: 'A hot ditty bawled by a *négresse soi-disant*', could not stop it stopping the show. But first she brought *Stormy Weather* to *Dark Doings* at the Leicester Square Theatre. She introduced Novello's *Shanty Town* and imported Piaf's *La Vie en Rose*. She alone kept *As Time Goes By* alive through the '30s until it was picked up by *Casablanca*.

She starred at the Palladium with Tommy Trinder during the war, and toured the big variety theatres. She entertained the troops in the Mediterranean with Edith Evans, John Gielgud and Beatrice Lillie. She was billed variously as 'Sepia Songstress', 'Syncopating Songstress' and even 'Mistress of Song', until she heard two gallery girls deduce that she was 'kept by a Chinaman'.

Her last big musical was *Pippin* (1973). In the '80s she was welcomed back to her home city in Bobby Short's *Black Broadway*, in David Kernan's *Kern Goes to Hollywood* and in her one-woman show which she took to Russia, singing for audiences of 4,000, across Australia and all over Britain.

She gave herself tirelessly to AIDs relief fund-raising concerts, retiring to Denville Hall only in her 90s, loved and admired for her warmth, elegance and fun, for her classically clear enunciation of a lyric, her exquisite musical taste and her gift for friendship. She liked to close rehearsals, conversations, even arguments, with a simple 'Amen'.

'Amen, Lis.'

Sir Paul Getty, KBE

1932-2003

Westminster Cathedral

Dame Thora Hird, DBE

1911-2003

Westminster Abbey

WHAT A WEEK IN Westminster! Cardinal Cormac Murphy-O'Connor's homily valiantly took on the text, 'It is easier for a camel to go through the eye of a needle than for a rich man to enter the Kingdom of God.' Getty, he emphasised, was 'exceedingly rich'. He found his answer in the next sentence: 'What is impossible with men is possible with God.' Jesus, he reminded us, had no particular animus towards the rich. On his journey to humility Sir Paul recognised that his fortune was not to be hoarded but shared. 'Despite much suffering, he retained a deep generosity, a desire to be of help and service to others.'

Christopher Gibbs outlined the inspiration for his action. 'His love of England was a romantic's, rooted in the movies and the literature. It was about freedom, courtesy and honour.' Cricket, films and the BFI, the Tory party, opera, bibliophilia and *The Oldie* were enthusiasms which drew like minds and beneficiaries to the Cathedral. They heard of Getty's often tragic life and his troubled relations with his father. 'There is a difference between liking and loving. Paul loved his father.'

DAME THORA'S SERVICE OPENED, joyously, with the glorious, thunderous 'oompahs' of a Salvation Army band. The Archbishop of York read 'For everything there is a season', and Greg Dyke 'Do not let your hearts be troubled', before he went on to chat up Lord Hutton. Thora's Tormé grandchildren spoke a delightful tribute in exotic Californian accents. Victoria Wood prefaced her reading with a suggestion that a stairlift should have carried her up to the high pulpit.

Alan Bennett followed in fine form. Thora was 'an actress', not that politically correct thing, 'a female actor'. She respected the text to the last 'and' and 'but'. In a rare improvisation in *A Kind of Loving*, the written line, 'You filthy, disgusting pig!' did not cover the time taken by Alan Bates to be comprehensively sick. Still on script, Thora mined every permutation on the four words. 'Lear over Cordelia was not more grief-stricken than Mrs Rothwell in her desecrated parlour.' Comics sometimes make the band laugh. 'Thora could make a camera crew cry.' She 'peaked' in her 70s and 80s, 'going on long enough to be taken seriously'. Her only rival in 'relentless reminiscence'? Sir John Gielgud.

Confused at the end, she told her daughter, Janette, that she was in a studio filming with John Wayne; but he had left the set.

'Look out of the window, Mum. Can't you see the mews?' Thora (doubtfully): 'Yes, but they can do wonders with scenery these days.'

Thora never expected to play Cleopatra, but brilliantly Bennett finished with Charmian's lament for the Egyptian queen: 'Now boast thee, death, in thy possession lies a lass unparalleled.'

A Lancashire Lass.

Peter Bromley
1929-2003
St Bride's Church, Fleet Street

Alexander Walker
1930-2003
St Bride's Church, Fleet Street

John Richard Schlesinger
1926-2003
Liberal Jewish Synagogue, St John's Wood

AN EMBARRASSMENT OF RICHES in these farewells. First the eulogies. Of Peter Bromley, Clare Balding recalled his advice, 'Never eat prawns the night before a race; look after your voice; always leave before the last race.' His daughter Lizanne saw him as 'a frustrated cowboy'. Ian Robertson witnessed him failing to wangle a special parking space for the Arc at Longchamps: 'Watch while I disarm them with my charm'; and, not having fired a pistol for 30 years, finding a team of crack SAS shots' near perfect score 'eminently beatable'. And beating it.

Roger Schlesinger remembered childhood visits to the Synagogue which brother John prophetically called 'the Cinemagogue'. He eased piano lessons by persuading his teacher, Kreisler's accompanist, to show off himself. His best infant acting? Shamming injury to be carried off the rugby field. Jim Clark, often John's editor, saw him deal with difficult actors. 'Do it your way, dear; but don't forget, we have the scissors.' He tangled happily with his long-time producer, Joe Janni:

'You are a 'omosexual. What-a-you know of women?'

'A lot more than you, you wily old Milanese philanderer!'

Prince of eulogists Alan Bennett was back with 'It's not often you can reprise a memorial address...' (see previous *Oldie* Schlesinger/Thora Hird story). He quoted Coral Browne, 'Don't worry, dear. John can always bring a crown of thorns out from under the bed'; and the Queen, adjusting his CBE ribbon, 'Now, Mr Schlesinger, we must try to get this straight.' John took it as a coded acknowledgment.

Max Hastings and Brian Forbes reminded us of Alex Walker's integrity and independence: 'He kept the flame of informed criticism alight, never smart-arsed, never snide'; his censorship battles, and the cupboards of tinned food he hoarded in case of an atomic attack.

For John, Joanna Lumley read Wordsworth and Stevenson, Alan Bates a sonnet. More Wordsworth ('splendour in the grass') from Joanna David for Alex. St Mark on the value of sight from Lord Rothermere and Dryden's *Happy the Man* – Sam West. A wonderful find at St Bride's: Peter Bromley's favourite, Banjo Patterson's 'In fact the race was never run on sea or sky or land/But what you'd get it better done by Riders in the Stand.'

And the music? Exquisite psalms by rich Jewish voices in St John's Wood, along with Mozart's '*Soave sia il vento*'. At St Bride's a heartfelt soloist for *O mio babbino caro* and variously Hupfeld's *As Time Goes By*, Porter's *Every Time We Say Goodbye* and Berlin's *Top Hat*.

We left St John's Wood thinking of John Schlesinger's family and his devoted partner, Michael Childers; St Bride's with the Trumpet Voluntary from *The Gadfly* tally-hoing Peter Bromley aloft; and the next night with Alex Walker's answerphone sign-off: '...And remember, smoking is the slow way to suicide.'

PETER BROMLEY
ALEX WALKER
JOHN SCHLESINGER

Sir Denis Thatcher Bt, MBE

1915-2003

The Guards Chapel

IT WOULD BE HARD to think of a service more suited to the man whose life was celebrated. Short – 40 minutes. Hymns: familiar and sturdy – *To Be a Pilgrim*, *I Vow to Thee My Country*, *Lead us Heavenly Father*, *Praise My Soul the King of Heaven*. Singing: beautifully rendered by the choir of the Guards Chapel, Director Tim Horton. Purcell's *Thou Knowest, Lord, the Secrets of our Hearts*. *The Chorus of Hebrew Slaves*, which Denis joyously and privately conducted whenever he heard it. Brahms' *How Lovely are thy Dwellings* and Tallis' *Salvator Mundi*. The Regimental Band of the Irish Guards, stirring throughout, lending their musician for Last Post and *Reveille*. The service shared between Padre Andrew Totten, Guards Chaplain, and Rev Richard Whittington, Royal Hospital, the other London chapel where the Thatchers often worshipped.

The Order of Service was prefaced with Tagore's *Farewell, my Friends*. Cecil Parkinson read Psalm 121, 'I will lift up mine eyes to the hills'; Stephen Tipping, Stevenson's 'The man is a success who has lived well, laughed often and loved much', and Lady Wakeham, Kipling's *L'Envoi*: 'When the earth's last picture is painted...'. Master Michael Thatcher, grandson, who was to lead his grandmother from the church, confidently lowered his microphone after the taller Parkinson and read from Thessalonians, 'And the dead in Christ will rise first', with great clarity, his accent hardly betraying an American timbre except on the single word 'Gahd'.

The eulogist was delightfully inevitable – Bill Deedes. 'Denis Thatcher was the most straightforward and forthright of men, who'd deplore any false note struck in his memory... Let me start by saying he was, in real life, a vast improvement on the *Private Eye* model. This was an altogether more considerable figure than those spoof letters to 'Dear Bill' led so many to

suppose. Not that I've got anything against th[...]
marvellously camouflaged his value to the Prime [...]
off his trail – that's my profession he was kind enoug[...]
And those letters made me famous. Well, sort of fa[...]
golf and gin went into the making of Denis Thatcher.

He remembered the soldier; the businessman who [...]
sheet; the loyal consort who gave up his beloved Rolls [...]
party's image-makers; and the host at Number 10, 'makin[...] nobody
felt left out... "Chancellor, meet Mrs Sims of Sudbury..." Lucky Chancellor!'
And he recalled the judge of character: 'Denis, what do you make of Bloggs?'
'Bloggs? Bill, he couldn't pull the skin off a rice pudding.'

'So let us pray that the Lord's merciful hand may stretch out to Margaret,
console her, bring her peace of mind... Denis left something imperishable.
He left us the memory of a character, a stamp of man, straight and true, to
which every father, whether soldier, man of business, sportsman or reptile,
might dearly wish their sons to aspire and if possible attain.'

Robert Louis Stevenson
*The man is a success who has lived well, laughed often, and loved much;
who has gained the respect of intelligent men and the love of children;
who has filled his niche and accomplished his task; who leaves the world
better than he found it, whether by an improved poppy, a perfect poem, or
a rescued soul; who never lacked appreciation of earth's beauty or failed to
express it; who looked for the best in others and gave the best he had.*

Rosemary Ackland
1929-2002
Dr Julia Trevelyan Oman, CBE
1930-2002

Both at St Paul's Church, Covent Garden

TWO WIDOWERS DEVISED IMPECCABLE celebrations of their wives' special gifts, offered with equal love in personal, appropriately different styles.

Joss Ackland's hymn to Rosemary was accompanied by seven children, 31 grandchildren and two great-grandchildren. Although it is unusual for the bereaved to be the principal eulogist, no one else could have done it. He recalled their romance. Children. Poverty. A defeated retreat to tea planting in Malawi. South Africa. A radio adaptation of *Black Beauty* which fell foul of apartheid! Return to Britain. A gynaecologist's verdict: Rosemary must conceive within 24 hours. Her dash to Pitlochry. Nine months later their just reward. Better days. Joss at the Mermaid. Then their house burnt down. Alone, Rosemary saved the children and threw herself from a window. Miraculously, pregnant again, she and the child survived the broken bones. The death of a beloved son. The word 'soul-mate' threaded the address. Her strength, struck down by the cruel assaults of motor-neurone disease. 'I race around in my dreams and I wake up in this miserable bag of bones.'

John Mortimer added grace notes. Claire Bloom and Greta Scacchi read from Rosemary's diary, cueing in heartache songs, *They Can't Take That Away From Me* and *My Cup Runneth Over*, beautifully sung by Liz Robertson and Robert Meadmore. All through, the excited rainbow children from the Centre of Young Musicians, singing '*Malawi mtima wansangala wa Africa*', written by Andrew Pratten in Blantyre, Malawi.

A MONTH LATER, WE heard how Roy Strong and Julia Trevelyan Oman eloped in 1971 to create scholarly achievement, theatre magic and a glorious garden, The Laskett. From it Sir Roy laid a sheaf of rosemary on the altar.

We sang the hymn of Harvest Home, *We Plough the Fields and Scatter*, a rarity at memorial celebrations – as was Francis Potts' *Angel Voices, ever Singing*. The herb rosemary and the flower honeysuckle had a significance for the couple which Sir Roy revealed, reading from his book about The Laskett. Patrick Garland spoke Marvell's *The Garden* – 'A green thought in a green shade.'

Music and Sir John Tooley's address evoked Julia's theatrical triumphs. Among them were *Brief Lives* – Alan Bennett read the evocative set description – and unique opera and ballet designs. He praised her dedicated research. He had visited The Laskett a few weeks before Julia's death and witnessed 'the couple's calm acceptance and planning of the service'. Sir John's address did eloquent justice to a remarkable woman and exemplary marriage.

***We Plough the Fields and Scatter** (M Claudius)*
We plough the fields and scatter, the good seed on the land,
But it is fed and watered by God's almighty hand:
He sends the snow in winter, the warmth to swell the grain,
The breezes and the sunshine, and soft, refreshing rain.

All good gifts around us are sent from heaven above;
Then thank the Lord, O thank the Lord,
For all his love.

Lord Rayne
of Prince's Meadow

1918-2003

The Olivier Theatre

HOW COULD SHE CELEBRATE the crowded life of Max Rayne in 90 minutes? Jane, Lady Rayne, solved it brilliantly. She filled the Olivier Theatre, there partly due to her husband, with so many Greats and Goods that one WMD would have eliminated Britain's artistic and financial establishment at a go.

Max's support for British Lion Films and the RADA was praised by Dickie Attenborough. His chairmanship of Festival Ballet prompted a lyrical dance tribute from Agnes Oaks and Thomas Edur. Richard Eyre detailed the National Theatre's debt for his shrewd handling of the move into the new building. And there was Max's wise warning that inevitably Richard would be 'absorbed by the establishment... wearing a leather jacket does not make you a revolutionary.'

Passionate support for opera was acknowledged by a young singer, Alice Coote, with a seasoned accompanist, Roger Vignolles. The Menuhin School provided players from France, Ireland, Wales, Romania and Iceland for Schumann's Piano Quintet, and that inspiring collection of children of all abilities, Lady Rayne's special enthusiasm, the Chicken Shed Company, erupted on stage as a climactic act.

Public achievements were matched by personal memories. Nicholas Rayne, on behalf of his siblings, lightened his proud recollections with a story of admiring an Air France hostess, to find, as they left the plane, his father giving him her phone number. 'I never called her. I don't think he did either.'

Jane read the Yeats poem that sealed their first meeting. Max knew it all, she only, 'Tread softly because you tread on my dreams'.

Lady Panufnik spoke of Max's bewilderment during the long time his Polish father took to return from World War I. 'Are you my father?' he would ask passers-by. It is wiser on these occasions to read rather than memorise a eulogy.

Dame Margaret Turner-Warwick extolled the Rayne Foundation, set up when Max was 44 to further his wish to allow artistic people to *begin* things.

Lord St John of Fawsley, sandwiched between the ebullient Chicken Shedders and the emotive Gregori Schechter Klezmer Trio, characterised the Hampstead home, Westfield, as simultaneously 'family fortress and Open City', and Max as 'unsparing in time and wisdom'. Presented with a mezuza after opening an exhibition of Jewish art, Norman asked Max if he should pin it to his door.

'One of your co-religionists used to touch a mezuza every day,' said Max.

'Oh, who was that?'

'Jesus.'

Denis Quilley, OBE

1927-2003

St Paul's Church, Covent Garden

To ANYONE DENYING THAT Denis Quilley was one of the best-loved actors of his generation, I throw down 'my gage'. Or if, as once happened to Denis playing Bolingbroke at the National, I forget to bring my gage on with me, I appeal to the overcrowded congregation at St Paul's for confirmation by acclamation. And I shall get it.

Kindly, Canon Bill Ritson, understudying Mark Oakley, found me a vestry chair at the back. Peter Hall praised these church visits as chances to see one's friends and do a bit of casting. He defined Denis as a perfect actor and lamented the layman's misconceived idea of self-obsessed creatures diminished by pejoratives like 'luvvies' and 'drama queens'. Denis was a 'drama monarch', a leading player who put the play and the team above himself.

Stella Quilley read Denis' favourite, *Loveliest of Trees*. Ronald Pickup chose a speech from Fry's exquisite *The Lady's Not for Burning*. Denis and Stella made their West End debuts in it. During the run they married. According to his autobiography, *Happiness Indeed* (launched after the service), her first line was, 'Hallo – can I have your telephone number?'

Denis grinned lasciviously: 'Oh yes!'

'No, no,' she disabused him. She was doubling as ASM.

Wendy Toye, who directed Denis on three early occasions, remarked on his versatility and his bicycle clips. Maureen Lipman, scattering laughter, remembered walks on Hampstead Heath and playing Second Randy Woman to him in *Tyger*. She banished it with: 'I thought I knew Denis well. Last year he did something entirely out of character. He died.'

Tim Pigott-Smith, who cast him as Pizarro in *The Royal Hunt of the Sun*, compared him to 'a good red Rioja'. When he asked for a more obviously antisocial character, Denis reflected, 'That may take some time.' But it came. Julia Mackenzie delivered her definitive *By the Sea* from *Sweeney*

Todd. Peter Reeves ferreted out a Michael Flanders poem, '*Afterword*', so witty and unfamiliar that it should be in every anthology – 'My days are so numbered...'

Michael Blakemore, who was, perhaps, Denis' preferred director, had noticed the flowers with which he graced his hotel rooms and shared a ridiculous, mysterious, mutual running joke: '...or a meringue'. Liz Robertson's *Wouldn't it be loverly?* was loverly. Bernard Hunter – colleague in 1953, agent since 1969 – spoke Coward's *When I have fears'* Simon Russell Beale celebrated Denis' Prospero (in the Regent's Park) and Imelda Staunton movingly reprised '*I Won't Send Roses'* from *Mack and Mabel* with Denis' recorded voice. Happily Mabel Normand's great-nephew, Stephen Normand, of the parish of St Paul's, was there to hear it ('...or a meringue').

Stewart Steven

1935-2004

St Bride's, Fleet Street

FLEET STREET'S FINEST TURNED out for Stewart Steven, augmented by the Blairs and Michael Heseltine. Lord Rothermere reads passages from the Scriptures at services for ex-employees – this time *Psalm 23*. One day he will have known them long enough to eulogise them. For the moment that task fell to Michael Howard and Matthew Norman.

Howard's address was an admiring, humorous, affectionate and self-deprecating tribute from the QC. Steven's mother wanted him to be a lawyer. He demurred: 'I could never understand why she should think so lowly of me.' The child of refugees, Jewish father and Lutheran mother, dad died young and mum sent him to an English public school hoping to turn him into 'the epitome of an English country gentleman'. Years later the English country gent would phone in to local radio stations as 'Clive of Chiswick' and commend to listeners 'a marvellous story in the *Mail on Sunday*'.

Long ago, in a one-day wonder most of us had forgotten, Howard's 18-year-old son, Nick, sent the *Evening Standard* an article headed 'Why an 18-year-old should not vote Labour'. Thanks to a mix-up it was published under Brian Gould's byline. Howard Senior and Steven remained friends.

Stewart Steven's passion for the arts and his cheek were celebrated. Imagine going up to Al Pacino and saying, 'How do you cope with being told you look like me?' Robin Esser read a witty wartime memory of Steven's involving Ritchie Calder, a white feather, brown shoes, spying and 'Careless Talk Costs Lives' (*Mail on Sunday*, 31 March 2002). Matthew Norman considered speaking his whole address in his old boss' voice. Briefly and hilariously he proved he could have brought it off. He went on to characterise Steven as an 'inspired, passionate, clever, witty, fearless, brilliant editor'.

Peter Bowles read *Sonnet 71* beautifully, introducing it with the story of Stewart's proposal to his widow, Inka, on her return from a visit to her native

Poland. He gave her a large, gift-wrapped box. It contained invitations to their imminent wedding – of which she was unaware. 'Send them to your family and friends,' he said. 'I've already sent mine.'

Two handsome, exotically clad youngsters, Nadeah Miranda and Art Menuteau, performed their song, *For You*. St Bride's Choir was at its impeccable best; most moving in *Thank You For Your Love*, a 40-year-old song by Inka Stevens written when she was a Polish pop star.

Sonnet 71 (William Shakespeare)
No longer mourn for me when I am dead
Then you shall hear the surly sullen bell
Give warning to the world that I am fled
From this vile world, with vilest worms to dwell:
Nay, if you read this line, remember not
The hand that writ it; for I love you so
That I in your sweet thoughts would be forgot
If thinking on me then should make you woe.
O, if, I say, you look upon this verse
When I perhaps compounded am with clay,
Do not so much as my poor name rehearse.
But let your love even with my life decay,
Lest the wise world should look into your moan
And mock you with me after I am gone.

Milton Shulman

1913-2004

Mortlake Crematorium

Hubert Gregg

1914-2004

St Paul's Church, Covent Garden

NICOLA NORMANBY TENDERLY SANG 'Whispering Milt's' bedtime song for his kids, Irving Berlin's *Russian Lullaby*. We left to the Ink Spots' *Java Jive*. Hubert Gregg's service was happily awash with his music. We all (including the Pearly Queen of the Old Kent Road and the Pearly King of Thornton Heath) joined in *Londoner*. Star duettists Louise Gold and Robert Meadmore finished their nostalgic medley with 'I'm gonna get lit up...', object of protests in the House by Lady Astor who considered it an incitement to drunkenness and riot.

Readings: Shulman's old colleague Herbert Kretzmer (after private coaching from Sir Ian McKellen) brought a touching simplicity to '*Our revels now are ended*'. David Jacobs read Gregg's memories of Bournemouth pierrots with songs – *When It's Nighttime In Italy, It's Wednesday Over Here* – and recitations – 'A marrow's a cucumber's father/A marrow's a cucumber's dad./It started off life as a gherkin/So it hasn't done so bad.' After a sonnet, Robert Gregg's moving postscript revealed how his father 'loved and corrected' his glottal stop. Richard Pascoe gave Hamlet's Advice to the Players, ruefully recalling Gregg's skilful lessons on playing comedy: 'Sadly, I'm not often asked!' Geoffrey Palmer pricelessly echoed his friend's recording of *Three Men in a Boat*.

Addresses: For Shaughan Seymour Hubert Gregg was 'witness to an age'. Alexandra Shulman remembered telling the time from the sounds of her father's early morning progress, his driving, learnt in a Sherman tank, his tennis, 'robbing Drobny of a set', and the apt-to-be-late critic's near-last words: 'Hurry, hurry! Where are the tickets?' Valerie Grove is getting too good at these eulogies: 'He could have been Bing Crosby if it hadn't been for the hay fever.'

Our Revels Now Are Ended *(William Shakespeare)*
Our revels now are ended. These our actors,
As I foretold you, were all spirits and
Are melted into air, into thin air:
And, like the baseless fabric of this vision,
The cloud-capp'd towers, the gorgeous palaces,
The solemn temples, the great globe itself,
Yea, all which it inherit, shall dissolve
And, like this insubstantial pageant faded,
Leave not a rack behind. We are such stuff
As dreams are made on, and our little life
Is rounded with a sleep.

Andrew Robert Buxton Cavendish, 11th Duke of Devonshire, KG, PC, MC

1920-2004

Guards Chapel

THERE WAS NO ADDRESS at Andrew Devonshire's stately Service, but all the Cavendish bases were touched. The Mayor of Eastbourne read *Sussex (By the Sea)*: 'And here the sea fogs lap and cling/And here, each warning each,/The sheep bells and the ship bells ring/Along the hidden beach.' A Trustee of the Chatsworth Settlement read from *Corinthians*, Sir Michael Rose, Colonel, Coldstream Guards, from *Ecclesiastes*. Buxton got a mention in the Bidding and the Anthem was set by Ireland – a nod, perhaps, towards Lismore.

The prayers encompassed the man's life. *A Countryman's Prayer* gave thanks 'for joy that men of goodwill, working together for the good of the countryside, find by their love of open air with horse and hound and rod and gun and sail'. The Soldier's Prayer, 'To fight and not to heed the wounds'. The Garter Prayer, which calls on God to save, not only 'Our Gracious Sovereign' but also 'all the Companions, living and departed, of the Most Honourable and Noble Order of the Garter'. Finally, the Collect of the Coldstream Guards: 'Let them ever be second to none in their devotion to their God, their Queen and their Country'.

The Grand March from *Aida* and 'Figaro', the Regimental Slow March, prepared us for a 'British' song medley by American songwriters. Vivaldi's

Concerto for Two Trumpets and Old Coldstream Marches as we left the Chapel completed the Band's contribution, apart from boosting the hearty singing of some favourite hymns.

Parson Heber's perfect paraphrase of *Revelations*, 'Holy, Holy, Holy!', fitted St Ambrose's requirements for a good hymn precisely: 'praising and attempting to explain the inexplicable'. The poor singing Parson suffered from psoriasis, like Potter's Singing Detective. Not so Mrs Ward Howe, whose *Mine Eyes Have Seen the Glory* is an ingenious amalgam of *Isaiah* and Macaulay, with a dash of *Genesis* – 'Crush the serpent with his heel' – and the *Song of Solomon* – 'In the beauty of the lillies Christ was born across the sea'. The apocalyptic vision of St John the Divine is peppered up by Mrs Howe's vivid experience the afternoon before she wrote the hymn. She had witnessed the Battle of the Potomac, where she saw 'men being killed by cannon and musketry, bayonet and sword'. Her hymn rapidly swept America and then the world. For its outright sale she received four dollars.

The Service closed with John Ellerton's apt verses from his hectic period of composition between 1870 and 1871: *The Day Thou Gavest Lord is Ended*, with their association 'with the end of a day, of a life, of the immutability of the Church and the impermanence of the earthly'.

The Duke's life has also been celebrated at Chatsworth and Lismore, perhaps with fewer members of the Royal Family or their representatives but doubtless with no less affection.

Norman Platt, OBE

1920-2004

St Paul's Church, Covent Garden

Admiral of the Fleet the Lord Hill-Norton, GCB

1915-2004

St Martin-in-the-Fields

NORMAN PLATT'S FAREWELL WAS admiring, affectionate and above all musical – as you would expect for the great architect of Kent Opera. No time was wasted on hymns. Peter Hill-Norton had planned his service in detail. It was a no-nonsense reflection of the great man. Nicholas Holtam, Vicar of St Martin, confirmed this. Was there a hint of disappointment in his preamble to the Bidding? 'A rather basic naval service,' he said.

Certainly it was triumphant. The Navy's church was awash with a sea of sailors. Hill-Norton's grandchildren processed his Orders and Decorations. The Band of Her Majesty's Royal Marines played us stirringly in and out. The sturdy hymns sang the Admiral's epitaph: 'Tranquil you lie, your knightly virtue proved,/Your memory hallowed in the land you loved'; The golden evening brightens in the West;/Soon, soon to faithful warriors cometh rest'; and, of course, William Whiting's eternal naval anthem, happily not the ghastly Evangelical rewrite but the real thing: 'Oh hear us when we cry to thee/For those in peril on the sea'. Even the French have adopted it: *'Vois nos pleurs, entends nos sanglots/Pour ceux en péril sur les flots'*. One Evangelical version actually commits: 'Oh hear us when we cry to you,/For those who sail the ocean blue'. Would that the same respect had been accorded the First Lesson, *I Corinthians* chapter 13, where 'charity' was sadly hijacked by 'love' again.

Admiral Sir Alan West is the First Sea Lord. (My latest measure of ageing is to notice that even First Sea Lords are looking younger.) He did a fine job of evoking the distinguished, peppery senior sailor. 'Ministry of Defence. Hill-Norton speaking. Kindly state your business. We are busy men here.' And, 'Knott does not understand defence and shows no inclination to learn'; 'Portillo is a little creep'. Proud of sitting in Nelson's stall in Westminster Abbey; NATO; curiously fascinated by UFOs later in life; and, at home, 'a rock', a daughter-in-law said. 'A rock can be uncomfortable when bumped into,' observed a son.

Our music critic should have reviewed Norman Platt's programme, which took its text from John Donne: 'No noise, nor silence, but one equal music'. Bach, Schubert, Pelham Humphry and Mozart were beautifully performed. Britten was represented by a Platt favourite, the exquisite setting of Hardy's *The Choirmaster's Burial*: 'As soon as I knew that his spirit was gone...' (James Oxley, tenor; Gary Cooper, piano).

Nicholas Hytner with his customary authority identified the director and conductors who owed a start to Norman Platt, who 'didn't look like the leader of an opera company ought to look'. They included Jonathan Miller, directors of the RSC, the National, Rambert, and Roger Norrington. 'He was wise and good and great... I respected him more than anyone I ever worked for.' His credo? 'The only thing that counts in music is quality.'

Norris McWhirter, CBE

1925-2004

St Martin-in-the-Fields

Alistair Cooke, KBE

1908-2004

Westminster Abbey

NO PC BISHOP'S DISAPPROVAL was going to prevent *I Vow To Thee, My Country* from kicking off Norris McWhirter's service. Then Christopher Gill banged out *Ephesians*, announcing it with authority as 'Christ's Epistle'. Ben Castle improvised delightfully around Elgar, Gershwin and the *Record Breakers* theme – a programme shared between his father and the McWhirters. Sir Roger Bannister recalled Norris' help in his four-minute mile and his selfless volunteering for a medical experiment on a treadmill, the physical equivalent of running up Everest in six hours. Anna Nicholas considered delivering 'the world's longest eulogy', but rejected that for memories of practical jokes, of Monsieur Mangetout, who ate a Cessna light aeroplane, and a schoolmistress aged 110 who, asked if she saw any of her old pupils, told McWhirter, 'No, they're all dead.'

Tim Rice read from Ross, in which the bereaved twin remembered a public piano duet. Another parent turned unaware to McWhirter père: 'I thought they were going to hit one another.' The father replied, 'It's the first time they've got all through it.' Joining the Navy, only one proved colour-blind. Summoned back, the failure identified colour charts as 'magenta' and 'ultramarine'. The new examining officer deduced that this had confused the orderly. 'In future,' he prescribed, 'try not to be so exact.'

Alistair McWhirter testified to a passion for Mars bars, hatred of closed shops and Europe, the achievement of the Guinness Books, and an inquiry about the exact area of Jersey. McWhirter queried, 'Tide in or out?' The abiding message echoed the obituaries: 'Despite his politics, you couldn't help liking him.'

ALISTAIR COOKE RATED THE Abbey; the Stars and Stripes flew above it. As usual the Abbey did not let us down. The *coup de l'Abbaye* was a welcome from Cooke himself – a recording pirated from an awards ceremony he could not attend. 'I'm sure you expect me to say that I'm sorry not to be with you today. Well, on the whole I'm not sorry. Radio broadcasters should be heard and not seen.' Truth to tell, the addresses were unremarkable, though Peter Jennings, of ABC News, amusingly imagined Cooke relishing the honour: 'Ah, the Abbey, well...'

Music clinched the occasion. Cooke worshipped Handel and introduced Leonard Bernstein to the composer. So we had much satisfying Handel and Bernstein's electric Chichester Psalms. Jazz was the broadcaster's other passion. Jacqui Dankworth thrilled the great church with her exquisitely delicate jazz tracery around *Someone To Watch Over Me*.

Cooke's voice cued our exit: 'Choosing between the Big Bang and the Book of *Genesis* –"And God said, Let there be light, and there was light" – I'd plump for *Genesis*.' Thunder, lightning and the *Hallelujah Chorus*. What else?

Bernard Levin, CBE

1928-2004

St Martin-in-the-Fields

SANDWICHED BETWEEN THOSE HYMN-MAKERS to the commonality, Bunyan and Blake, the meat of Liz Anderson's beautifully chosen Order of Service was haunting music, three riveting readings and three fine eulogies.

The Duke Quartet played Mozart and Schubert; members of Conchord played Richard Blackford's *Portrait of Hans Sachs*, culled from Wagner especially to surprise Bernard at one of his beloved Wexford reunions before the cursed clouds of Alzheimer's descended.

In Ms Anderson's reading he explained why he had to write: 'Nor could I draw or paint. Or sing. Or teach. Or dig. Or drive. Or cook. Or plant. Or be a conjurer...' And the key advice: '"Levin, what you want to do is write." And I did.'

Dame Maggie Smith wittily judged a favourite poem, *Heaven* by A S J Tessimond. 'In the heaven of the god I hope for (call him X)/There is marriage and giving in marriage and transient sex... Marx talks to Plato, Byron wonders whether/There's some mistake. Wordsworth has found a hill/That's home. Here Chopin plays the piano still...'

Billie Whitelaw delivered Bernard's classic *Quoting Shakespeare*, with its staccato climax: 'By Jove! O Lord! Tut, tut! For goodness sake! What the Dickens! But me no buts... It's still all one to me, for you are quoting Shakespeare.'

The addresses split the life in three. Sir David Frost barnstormed back to TW3. On the pilot a Tory lady shouted more than once at Bernard, 'Mr Macmillan has always satisfied me!' and 'Mr Levin, how would you like it if your daughter was up a dark lane at night and nothing done about it?' Levin on British catering: 'If there is a word to describe it, and there is, it is "disgusting"'. His quest for hospitality in Glasgow: 'Where d'you think you are? On the Continent?' Sir Cyril (Hang 'em, Flog 'em) Osborne's addiction

to the Speaking Clock, panting for 'at the t
to fatuous correspondents: 'Dictated by E
presence by...' or 'I think I should warn you
gained possession of your writing paper.'

Long ago Bel Mooney was briefed by Ber
was not a damsel in distress he would not resc
affectionate, comprehensive and amusing. In a k
of all the ladies who loved him', she blew a kiss fr
caught that, dearest Bernard.'

Sir Simon Jenkins summed up Levin's genius a̱   ...ɑust and essayist.
On going off on a long walking tour he 'would leave behind six perfectly
crafted columns: two on the Wexford Festival, two on Montaigne and two
on the North Thames Gas Board.'

As Bernard was wont to say: 'The pen is mightier than the sword, and
much easier to write with.'

Sir Peter Alexander Ustinov

1921-2004

St Martin-in-the-Fields

THE BELLS OF ST MARTIN rang a jubilant greeting and the Order of Service printed laudatory messages from Boris Becker, Daniel Barenboim and Mikhail Gorbachev. Gorbachev described Peter as 'not only a gifted actor, prolific director, prominent producer and author, but also a remarkable, authentic person.' The penultimate word may have lost something in translation.

Welcoming us, the Rev Nicholas Holbann pointed out that Peter had not enjoyed his time at Westminster School, adding slyly, 'Perhaps that is why we are here today and not at the Abbey'. Terence Stamp, whose first starring role was Billy Budd, directed by Ustinov, introduced the familiar and appropriate passage from R L Stevenson ('He has achieved success who has lived well, laughed often and loved much...') by recalling wise advice at the end of shooting: 'He took me aside and said, "You will be offered lots of work. Remember, if you do good things, good things will come to you."'

The service was sprinkled with exquisite music. Steven Isserlis's playing of Bach's *Prelude* and *Sarabande* from his violoncello Solo Suite in D Minor BWV 1008 was, perhaps, the highlight.

Tamara Ustinov, with her husband Malcolm Rennie, performed a charming excerpt from her father's funny first hit play, *The Love of Four Colonels*. Nick Atkinson, a young actor whom Peter helped through drama school, delighted the congregation. 'I had seen him on television playing a Belgian detective and in my blue pyjamas I had been stunned into a state of bolt-upright hypnosis... At school, while my friends were planning how to lose their virginity in the Easter holidays, I was writing to a 68-year-old character actor – thankfully with a different agenda.' When he told Ustinov,

'My first agent had two Yorkshire terrier
looked suspicious but simply said, 'That's w
he represent them?'

William Pace concentrated on Peter's inva.
Federalist Movement and his role as Dean of UN
He leavened his address with memories of his se
through from 'Senator Jesse Helms' or 'President Jimi.
rumbled their impersonator.

Theodore Chapin read his indisposed father Schuyler's tu.   .inding
us of the passion for music, of the ability to imitate whole orcnestras and of
a rebuke to a suggestion that Frank Martin was the only Swiss composer.
Ustinov fired off the names of forty – all of whom proved to be in *Grove*.
Chapin had seen Peter's *Lear* in Canada: 'I've got three daughters of my own
– more preparation than Stanislavski ever had.'

Best of all, his response to a New York cabbie's 'Have a nice day':
'Thank you, but I have other plans.'

gel Nicolson, OBE, FRSL, FSA

1917-2004

The Guards' Chapel

I WOULD BE SURPRISED IF Nigel Nicolson did not have a hand in planning his own Service, so meticulously did it reflect his virtues, responsibilities and enthusiasms. If it was devised by his three children, who also took part, they did Papa proud.

No sooner had Rebecca Nicolson read the passage from Stevenson's *Success*, which also featured most recently at Peter Ustinov's service, than we embarked on a neatly arranged *Seven Ages of Man*, threaded through with a hymn, two anthems and the band of the Grenadiers' enthusiastic take on *Lili Marlene*.

Adam Nicolson covered the first age – The Son. One key was Nigel's admiration for his father: 'He lived, not in his father's shadow, but in his light.' His feelings for his mother, Vita Sackville-West, were more complex.

The second age was The Soldier, delivered by John Buchanan. In Tunisia Nicolson commandeered a clapped-out car, and was fascinated to observe a German surrender. The officers exhorted their men to maintain their discipline in captivity, whereupon they marched off smartly to cries of 'Ra! Ra! Ra! Sieg Heil' and the strains of *Lili Marlene* .

In Italy he was held in awe by his men for his historical knowledge, command of languages and his sensitivity amidst the cruelties of war. The Order of Service included his account of 'the most dramatic speech I ever made'. Addressing his audience of Guards in the mountains overlooking Cassino he alone knew that a barrage greater than that fired at El Alamein would start at precisely 11 pm. 'Having kept a close eye on my watch,' he timed his briefing to finish with 'You will want to know where and when this vast operation will begin – "Here," I cried, "And now!"' On cue, all hell broke loose.

Lord Mayhew praised The Politician whose stand over Suez was too much for Bournemouth Tories. Independent, principled, 'the stuff of Whips' nightmares'. Lord Weidenfeld, eponymous fellow publisher, recalled *Lolita*; threatened during a cruelly cold winter, but given a discreet Home Office nod which founded the firm's fortunes.

Eileen Atkins (an eloquent speaker who should do more of this work) traced Nigel's literary style to his father for his classical prose and to his mother for her observation. She taught him that 'nothing is really done until you describe it.'

Martin Drury, one-time Director General of the National Trust, took on the Sixth Age – The Man of Sissinghurst. One wet day in 1930, when Nigel was 13, his mother showed him the house for the first time, saying 'I think we shall be very happy here'. The boy replied, 'We don't have to live here, do we?' unaware of how his affection and delight would grow.

In the Seventh Age Juliet Nicolson remembered The Father. 'The best listener I ever met.' At the end he lay uncomplaining in the Tower, surrounded by pots full of cuttings. 'I shall not go to the garden again, so the gardener brings the garden to me.'

133

HRH Princess Alice, Duchess of Gloucester

1901-2004

St Clement Danes Church

Rt Hon Sir Nicholas Scott, KBE

1933-2005

Chelsea Old Church

POOR BLAMELESS PRINCESS ALICE. As I got into my taxi in the Strand, having negotiated the statues of Tedder and Harris which mount guard on the RAF Church, the driver asked, 'Who was that all about then?' 'Memorial service for the old Duchess of Gloucester,' I told him. 'Ah!' he said, alert at once. 'Was she the one years back with the 'eadless man?' 'No,' I disappointed him. 'That was poor guilty Margaret, Duchess of Argyll.'

Princess Alice's son, the Duke, who succeeded as a result of his brother's tragic death, delivered an impeccable eulogy. He was fortunate 'to have had a mother for so long, even if at 60 it seemed unusual to be without one.' (Shades of a weeping Clifton Webb famously 'orphaned at 70'.) He listed her birth on Christmas Day, her many Montague Douglas Scott siblings, her affection for Kenya, her involvement with the Air Force, and, 'as proof of her eccentricity, she married late'.

When very young she visited a fortune-teller who told her that she would marry 'above her station'. As third daughter of the Seventh Duke of Buccleuch, she permitted herself a superior smile. However, as her son wryly pointed out, 'Entering the Royal Family had all its mixed blessings.' He went on to celebrate the diplomat, the charity leader, the knitter, the embroiderer, especially the gardener and, touchingly, the vague centenarian visited in the last weeks of her life by her granddaughter, Davina. 'Why do I love you?' 'Because I am your granddaughter.' 'Ah, yes!'

SIR NICHOLAS SCOTT'S POPULARITY in Chelsea and in Parliament was confirmed by a solid turn out of locals and senior Tories. Most of them looked like Sir Peter Tapsell, though only one was – a grey-haired man, just too young, to paraphrase Baldwin, 'to have done very well out of the war'.

The Rev Dr Peter Elvy presided sympathetically as always. The choir sounded as good as usual. Sister Celine of the Nazareth Nursing Homes, where Sir Nicholas spent his last clouded years, led us in the *Lord's Prayer*. His four children played their parts in reading and lighting a candle.

Happy choices as eulogists, not from the top Tory table, were Peter Hughes, a school-friend who recalled their time at Clapham College (also Alma Mater of Germaine Greer's one and only husband) and Peter Samson, close to Sir Nicholas in his years of honours and service in Ulster. Both spoke of chivalry, loyalty and a passion for cricket.

His ashes rest 'in the Columbarium under Chelsea Old Church.' I had to look up 'Columbarium'. I don't think the Old Church sports a dovecote; so they must lie in 'a vault with niches for the reception of cinerary urns.' Rest in peace.

Dame Alicia Markova, DBE
1910-2004
The Rt Hon Sir Angus Ogilvy, KCVO
1928-2004

Both at Westminster Abbey

THEY WEREN'T DANCING IN the aisles at Dame Alicia's service, but they were in the Nave and the Lantern. The English National Ballet (of which she was President), direct descendant of Festival Ballet (which she co-founded), cast excellent English National dancers with exotic non-English names. Daria Klimentova, Dmitri Gruzdyev, Erina Takahashi and Arionel Vargas danced the Act Two *pas de deux* from *Giselle*; Agnes Oaks and Simone Clarke performed the prelude from *Les Sylphides*, all to applause.

'Lovely,' I heard one balletomane whisper, 'but they can't do the *demi-plié* after the *assemblée* like Alicia.'

Few prima ballerinas matched her, none touched her pioneering role in British ballet – as Sir Peter Wright pointed out. With Diaghilev, her direct early teenage influences included Fokine, Nijinska, Massine, Stravinsky and Matisse. After his death she danced for Marie Rambert.

Clement Crisp, in an elegant reading from *Markova Remembers*, switched the printed 'Miss' Rambert to the familiar 'Mim' and recorded Dame Alicia's historic, fog-threatened triumph in *Giselle*, the first classical cornerstone of the Vic-Wells Ballet, precursor of the Royal.

Sir Peter recalled the première of Ashton's *Façade*. She finished the demanding polka with a surprise double *tour en l'air*, hitherto reserved for men. He sensitively emphasised the part played by Sir Anton Dolin in Markova's career and his importance in the development of British ballet – a contribution far too often forgotten these days by later leading male dancers, none of whom have established the same starry rapport with the public.

After the Vic-Wells came the Markova-Dolin company, then America, Festival Ballet, then teaching, coaching and Presiding. Sitting in front of him at Covent Garden, Markova apologised for her 'famous Kabuki-style coiffure' – 'Please don't ask me to remove my hair.'

Young ballet students assisted the Rev Chris Chivers and Rabbi Roderick Young in the prayers. The Rabbi's rich voice resonated the *Eishet Chayil* with an appropriate passage from *Proverbs*: 'A woman of worth, who can find her, for she is more precious than rubies.'

THE PRAYERS FOR SIR Angus included offerings from two recipients of business start-up loans from the Prince's Trust, in partnership with Sir Angus' Youth Employment Scheme. An extract from his daughter Marina's theme music for *Engaged* preceded a moving address by her brother, James. Taking as his text Timothy West's impeccable reading of *If*, his father's favourite poem, James Ogilvy was able to highlight his courage, perseverance, modesty and especially his rapport with people: 'If you can talk with crowds...'

Sir Angus could. On his death, James Ogilvy received a letter of condolence from one of his teenage godsons. 'He was really cool, an utter legend.' Apparently he had been able to discuss both 'iPods and the model Jordan' with the letter-writer on equal terms.

hony Sampson
1926-2004
St Martin-in-the-Fields

WITH SIX IMPRESSIVE EULOGISTS and Janet Suzman's thoughtful reading of Shakespeare's 'Fear no more...' I had better 'cut to the cackle', which was excellent.

Hugh Thomas was up first. He had a lexicon of Anthonys: Johannesburg Anthony and *The Drum*; 'Anatomy' Anthony; Biographer Anthony; Anthony 'the fearless commentator railing against "the Dictator Blair"'; and a handful more before Beefsteak Anthony and Neighbour Anthony – an 'over the garden wall' friend who, as a journalist, very properly never accepted an honour.

Neal Ascherson recalled his Anthony at the height of his powers in Namibia and in his hilarious account of 'the only aeroplane that I have had to get out of and push'. Sampson gave Ascherson his *entrée* to the *Observer*. Here he studied his interviewing technique; the skilful, relentless listener, fixing an unflinching gaze on the interviewee and 'the genuine anger under the urbanity'.

Katie Sampson quoted Nelson Mandela's words to her brother: 'Paul, you chose your father well.' Mandela contributed a note to the Order of Service: 'He cared about Africa in a way that is rare in the developed world and he never stopped caring.' Ms Sampson announced an *Independent* award in her father's memory to foster South African journalists.

John Matshikiza, son of Todd and another part of the *Drum* legacy, was born in 1954. When Sampson flew back to England, the child was told to wave and call 'Goodbye, Uncle Tony!' For ages after, any plane passing over Orlando West produced the same wave and cry.

The choir sang a moving *Nkosi Sikelel iAfrica* and Paul Sampson read a passage from *The Scholar Gypsy*, his father's biography of his grandfather, Dr John Sampson, the Rai, or scholar, who published his *Oxford Dictionary of Romany Languages* in 1931. It described the scattering of his ashes nine times over a Welsh mountainside. One Welsh spectator was heard to exclaim 'Pity 'tis to scatter the ashes so, and give the Almighty all the work of collecting them together again.'

There is no more confident top of the bill than Tony O'Reilly, who spoke of 'this most English of Englishmen' with his 'socialist sense of constant enquiry and a search for justice'. He quoted the French statesman who flattered Palmerston – 'If I wasn't French I would wish to be English.' Palmerston replied, 'If I wasn't English I would wish to be English.' A tale of four seafood-selling brothers of Wexford confronted by the Heinz magnate had once provoked the question, 'Did we make a difference?' 'Anthony Sampson made a difference.'

We spilled out into Trafalgar Square warmed by a story of Brendan Behan after he had served some time in a clinic in West Cork. He enjoyed it. 'At this clinic the nurses and doctors drink with the patients – nobody gets cured, but the time does fly!'

from Cymbeline (William Shakespeare)
Fear no more the heat o' the sun,
Nor the furious winter's rages;
Thou thy worldly task hast done,
Home art gone, and ta'en thy wages;
Golden lads and girls all must,
As chimney-sweepers, come to dust.

The Lord Hanson
1922-2004
St Paul's, Wilton Place

Patsy Rowlands
1934-2005
St Paul's Church, Covent Garden

MY SCORE IN WILTON Place is now Two Weddings and a Memorial. The Great and the Good filled St Paul's for James Hanson. I even glimpsed one or two of the not-so-Good.

Sandwiched between the obligatory Bunyan and Blake were two metrical psalms, No 23, faithfully transposed by the Vicar of the Welsh Marshes, H W Baker, into *The King Of Love My Shepherd Is*, and No 137, much more ambitiously transformed as *Praise My Soul The King of Heaven* by that delicate bibliophile, the Perpetual Curate of Lower Brixham, H F Lyte, who was to pen *Abide With Me* on the morning he left Devon to die in Italy.

The Hon Lucas White wins Best Turned Out First Lesson Reader Award (*Corinthians* 13). More original and more relevant, Sir William Creasy read from Theodore Roosevelt: '*His place shall never be with those cold and timid souls to know neither victory nor defeat.*' Prayers were led by Lord Hope of Thornes, once Archbishop of York, now a happy, humble parish priest.

Lord Palumbo lingered on the Yorkshire connection. Apart from his love of that county, Britain and the United States ('irresistible', a passion shared with Gordon White), we heard of Lord Hanson's devotion to his wife, 'If she was his rock, he was her fortress'; his early life, 'A whiff of the Elizabethan buccaneer'; his response to anxious shareholders – a soothing personal phone call; his mistrust of 'the Nanny state' and his stance, 'faithful to friends, formidable to opponents'.

In Covent Garden we said goodbye to the delightful Patsy Rowlands and *au revoir* to the Rector, Mark Oakley, now 'Anglican Archdeacon of Germany and All Northern Europe' or, as he puts it, 'Führer of Copenhagen'. In the Bidding he cherished Patsy's work for Boggs Sanitary Ware in *Carry On at Your Convenience* ('I gave my life to Boggs'). Her last role was Mrs Pearce in *My Fair Lady*, its first scene set under the portico of the church in which we sat.

Warmth and affection pulsed through the building as son, ex-husband, colleagues and agent remembered her funny, dizzy unpunctual private life and her impeccable professionalism, whether selling Britvic fruit juice on a stand at the Ideal Home Show, or at the Players' Theatre, brilliantly taking Marie Lloyd's 'Morning Promenade', or in *Valmouth* floating 'I Loved A Man', happily recorded; her dogs, her painting and her 'World's Largest Collection of Plastic Bags'; 'She never threw anything away, from a new recipe for low-fat biscuits to a photograph of every dog ever taken.'

When her agent, Simon Beresford, rang to say she had been cast as Mrs Pearce, which she desperately wanted, he told her to write down 'Y.O.U.G.O.T.I.T.' She read it back. 'YOGHURT?' 'No, you got it!' 'What, yoghurt?' No, *My Fair Lady*!

'Two days before she died,' her son Alan said, 'she decided to retire. The next day she was planning a comeback!'

Sir John Mills, CBE

1908-2005

St Martin-in-the-Fields

THE RADA USHERED Sir John Mills' celebration. Squads of students in yellow T-shirts showed us in. One young man tried to banish me upstairs but a buxom RADA girl helped me to outwit him. The Vicar, Nicholas Holtam, said, 'Sir John could always pull in a good crowd.' And he did.

Maxwell Caulfield (son-in-law) kicked off with Philippians 4, thundering 'Rejoice in the Lord *alway*: And again I say Rejoice' in a resonant baritone which suggested he is wasted on the small screen. Lady Mills's *Whistle Down the Wind* has had a strange history. Keith Waterhouse and Willis Hall retold her story of Home Counties, pony-club children finding Jesus (a convict on the run) in a stable. They set the movie in the bleak Sixties north. Andrew Lloyd Webber shifted the credulous characters, now pubertal, to the American South. His score yielded the title song for the service, sensitively sung by Andrea Ross, accompanied by the composer.

Sir John rated five eulogies and contributions from his family. His godson, Michael Attenborough, testified to his determination 'to relish every single moment of his life right up to the end' – more relevant than the bit of the dreaded Prophet to which he treated us.

Stephen Fry confessed that he had done 'an unforgivable thing... for an Englishman... I wrote a poem.' He called it 'Johnny's Eyes', so struck had he been by the man behind those bright, albeit unseeing, blue eyes. It was charming. The Editor might like to solicit a copy for this magazine.

Judi Dench, who lit up a lack lustre *The Good Companions* with Sir John, found him 'the naughtiest man I ever met'. He took audible orders during the finale to Act One for an after-show supper at Overton's ('bottle of champagne and a large lobster') in case the kitchen closed. He added heavy stage weights to a suitcase to teach a recalcitrant actor a lesson. 'I have never seen such amateur behaviour in my life,' a senior actress told the two consummate professionals.

From The Family, daughters, grandsons and a great-granddaughter, we had an eloquent mixture of songs, poems and memories. 'His greatest performance: pretending not to be blind for the last few years.' His fondness for unrepeatable polar bear jokes. John Pudney's poem *Johnny-Head-in-Air* from the wartime film, *The Way to the Stars*. His favourite of Crispian Mills-Boulting's songs: *Shower Your Love On Me*. Stephen Fry was quoted in splendid summation: 'He was like a thread of tweed running through England.'

Donald Chilvers placed Sir John happily among his neighbours in Denham and praised his devoted assistant, Patricia Horrock. It was left to Richard Attenborough to call on 63 years of friendship and to remember Sir John's widow, Mary, 'who wrote exquisite plays for him and guided his choices'.

Daniel Frank Crawford

1942-2005

St Mary's, Islington

PERHAPS I SHOULD EXPLAIN who Dan Crawford was – a much-loved American who adored England. In 1970, on half-a-shoestring, he started the first pub 'dinner' theatre and battled to keep it open at the King's Head opposite St Mary's, where we buried him and celebrated his life.

He was lucky in his neighbour, Canon Dr Kings, whose sermon was better informed and crafted than many. He was aware of Tom Stoppard's verdict on Dan, 'Stark, raving sane', and the *Times*' accurate description, 'rumpled American'. He lamented Dan's death 'in the midst of the stress of nations', quoting comfortably from Eliot's *Four Quartets*: 'What we call the beginning is often the end / And to make an end is to make a beginning. The end is where we start from.'

The hymns were chosen by Dan and very 'Dannish' and Anglophile they were, including an outing, rare in these circumstances, for *God Save The Queen,* as well as *Jerusalem*; the optimistic *Look to the Rainbow* encompassing Dan's philosophy according to E Y Harburg, 'Follow the fellow who follows a dream'; and *Spread A Little Happiness*, sweetly sung by a much moved Janie Dee.

Benedict Nightingale remembered the boy from Hackensack who likened it to Croydon, 'but not so pretty', and his coming upon a pub 'so derelict even the winos ignored it'. Steven Berkoff boldly admired his conversion of 'a dingy pub into a dingy fringe theatre', the opportunities he gave him, 'the spine-wrenching seats' and the food. 'If you survived the pre-show dinner even the play seemed good.' Ann Pinnington's tribute recalled Dan's thrift-shop tweed clothes, never removed even on boiling Spanish beaches.

Lee Lawson read Stephanie Sinclair Crawford's tribute to 'Dan Quixote', Peter England the words of Dan's step-daughter, away in Africa. Dan's mother spoke movingly.

Maureen Lipman combined affection, admiration and fun in her unique fashion. Of the impresario, 'the names Lilian Bayliss, Sir Donald Wolfit, Dan Crawford and Max Bialystock spring to mind in no particular order.' When he promoted her appearance in Bernstein's *Wonderful Town* he sold her the part as 'the Cleopatra of musical roles' and advertised in the *Financial Times*, 'Bernstein and Lipman, Can You Believe It?' He greeted angels on Upper Street with one hand while painting scenery with the other. 'With frightening regularity,' she said, 'I've raised money for the King's Head.' Asked to view 'the new improvements... I was reduced to silence.'

She personified the emotions of the congregation. Sadly, she tactfully omitted a line she had considered about Dan's ever-present collecting cans: 'Every time I saw that famous bucket, I wondered when Dan was going to kick it!'

Ross Benson

1948-2005

St Bride's, Fleet Street

THE DAILY MAIL HONOURED its star war correspondent, Ross Benson, with a vivid supplement to his handsome Order of Service. It carried his reports from Baghdad, 'when the dogs began to howl' long before the stealth planes found their targets, when a limbless child screamed 'Mama!' but 'there was no mother to comfort her. Her mother was among the dead'; from Hong Kong when Prince Charles left the colony with the words, 'We shall not forget you'; and from a memoir of childhood when, in Sherwood Forest, he visited the grave of his old nanny who 'subscribed to the ancient belief that service to others was reward enough'.

The moving programme was topped and tailed by Sabine Baring-Gould's *Onward Christian Soldiers* and Lerner and Loewe's *Ascot Gavotte*, inspired bookends for a famous war reporter and flamboyant gossip columnist. His son, Dorian, read that beautifully short Indian prayer. Simon Williams was given what must have been a Ross favourite, *The Lake Isle of Innisfree*. Robert Powell did justice to a splendid extract from Tennyson's *Ulysses*. 'I cannot rest from travel: I will drink life to the lees', ending: 'The long day wanes; the slow moon climbs... Come my friends, 'tis not too late to seek a newer world.'

The choir of St Bride's were on top form. Lord Rothermere read the classic despatch from Baghdad. Paul Dacre (editor) reconciled Ross' faithful reporting of the 'filthy reality of war' while revelling in 'the reputation of a dandy-sculpted jacket nipped in at the waist, a wardrobe of handmade shoes to rival Imelda Marcos, pocket handkerchief always peeping elegantly from his top pocket.'

A second eulogist elaborated on Ross as 'Beau Benson... the acceptable face of vanity', remembering him affectionately as a young father spending Christmas at Hickstead Place, pondering, 'What shall I wear to push

Arabella's pram?' The earlier Beau (Brummell) had his boots 'cleaned in champagne'; Ross' were polished by a Buckingham Palace footman. One friend had thought that Benson was gesticulating at him through a restaurant window, only to realise that he was checking his hair in the glass. Conversely, the unshaven, unwashed, exhausted reporter, finally back at base, dutifully called his wife, Inge, to be told, 'It's all right for you, swanning around in Kosovo'. When he complained to his photographer, the photographer said, 'That's nothing, my wife's broken her nail!'

Then there was the story of recording Prince Charles' snores at Gordonstoun; Bob Geldof's accusation that he caught Ross in Africa blow-drying his hair with an aeroplane's propeller; and his six-year stint on Southern Television – 'The Cary Grant of Lewes.'

The Right Hon the Baroness Blatch of Hinchingbrooke, CBE

1937-2005

St Margaret's, Westminster

Jack Tripp, MBE

1922-2005

St Paul's Church, Covent Garden

IT WAS GOOD TO hear pleasant and positive things said of Emily Blatch, hitherto stamped in my memory as a blinkered, implacable advocate of the pernicious Section 28.

Lord Harris of Peckham told an endearing tale of lunching with her and a legendary Kent and England wicket keeper whom she confused with the restaurant in which they sat. To her it was French, *Les Ames*. John Major plainly adored her. Both men were full of admiration for her courage in her battle with cancer. Sir John's favourite rhetorical device is the repetition of a phrase; in this case 'Emily was there'. Be he candidate, MP, Prime Minister, or on the scrap-heap, 'Emily was there'.

'Did you ever know her not to have an opinion? Did you ever know her not to express it? Did you ever know her to be on time?' Besotted with her grandchildren, lucky in her husband ('He's a good listener'), we got a picture of a dedicated and formidable local and Parliamentary politician.

ST PAUL'S BUZZED WITH the brave vivacity of veteran Variety survivors celebrating the last of the great traditional pantomime dames.

Roy Hudd was a genial master of ceremonies with the Revd Katherine

Rumens (Barbican Arts) as a spirited 'Mrs Interlocutor'. Roy evoked the spirit of pantomime ('Tell me, Nurse Ribena, how old are you?' 'I'm approaching 38.' 'Indeed, from which direction?'), and Jack Tripp's occasional barb. He was told by Ivan Owen ('the hand up Basil Brush') that Owen's home had been burgled – 'but they didn't take anything.' 'Oh dear,' said Tripp. 'How humiliating!'

Joan Savage sang *The Sunshine of your Smile* ('Big finish coming up, Jack!') Bill Pertwee recalled The Fol de Rols. Roy Hudd had started a running carp at 'dodgy celebrities' in pantomime, and Judy Spiers confessed to being one. Jonathan Cecil once told Tripp that he didn't think one such 'was too bad'. 'Well,' said the resigned Dame, 'at least he was boring.'

Perhaps some testimonies were more about the speaker than the subject but affection and admiration shone through. Cecil first saw Tripp at 15 playing Johnny, Mother Goose's son, to Ethel Revnell's Dame. He marvelled at three speciality turns – aged ballerina, raw recruit with rifle, and a lightning tap routine. Later, he saw him in his rightful role ('I am now going in to the Supper Room to triffle with the trifle'). Dame Durden, Sarah the Cook, Mrs Crusoe, Widow Twankey, 'he was not in love with himself but he was in love with his craft... Eternally young, his sense of magic untarnished, the irrepressibly droll Jack Tripp embodied the true comic spirit of Christmas past, present and future.'

Oh, yes he did.

Willis Hall

1929-2005

St Paul's Church, Covent Garden

CANON ROGER ROYLE URGED us to regard the service as 'an extended Grace before a long lunch'. Grace began with *While Shepherds Watched* to the tune of *On Ilkley Moor Baht'at*! Did Willis know the words of the carol were by Nahum Tate? He also wrote *A Treatise on Syphilis* and a happy ending to *King Lear*, and he died hiding from his creditors in the Royal Mint.

Michael Parkinson, first up, thought that the shotgun marriage of words and music 'promised more than it delivered'. He also chided the good Canon for limiting Willis' sporting enthusiasms to cricket and rugby league, excluding 'Fairy Football'. Willis loved the terraces, even when he had access to the Directors' Box.

He and Parky collaborated on a football book. In fact, Willis wrote not a word. His 'collaborator' suggested that at least he contribute a foreword, 'saying what a joy I am to work with'. 'Willis was a man of few words, unless he was paid for them. Then you couldn't stop him!' There was a vignette of another service, a funeral. Woman to Willis: 'Was 'e poorly?' Willis: 'If he wasn't, we've buried the wrong man.'

Geoffrey Bayldon read from *The Exquisite Garden*, a favourite book to which he introduced Willis. George Stiles accompanied James Gill for *Breathe*, one of his warmly remembered collaborations with Willis, who once told him of a pie competition among Yorkshire butchers, 'as grand a band of chaps as ever assembled in an abattoir'.

James Hall's filial tribute was as simple, stylish and loving as these things should be. 'In his last 10 years he didn't drink. He still lunched. It wasn't the drink he craved. It was the company.'

Harry Taub and Denis King did spirited justice to *The Old Triangle* which Willis, when in high spirits, sang in three different keys.

If I have failed to convey the overwhelming warmth of this unique evocation of a much-loved man, I call Keith Waterhouse. His slow assisted progress to the lectern was concluded by the request, 'Pick me up at about four o'clock'. His affectionate eulogy was punctuated by a senior moment. 'I know what I'm going to say... it's just that I've forgotten... [long pause]... Oh yes, films. We wrote films.' They also wrote 'scripts while you wait, success not guaranteed.' One, which they wrote for TW3, beautifully summed up the Northerner's ironic amusement at fashionable success in the Swinging South in the '60s.

'Life has been good to the Northerner. He had nothing to say and they called him dour. He had a vocabulary of 450 words and they praised his plain speaking. He was rude, coarse and pig-ignorant and they called him blunt.'

The Right Hon Robin Finlayson Cook, MP

1946-2005

St Margaret's, Westminster

THERE WERE SOME PUZZLING Royal Representatives at Robin Cook's service. Who, I wondered, could be standing in for the Queen and the Duke as 'Lord Evans of Temple Guiting'? And who was the Prince of Wales' understudy, 'Baroness Smith of Gilmorehill'? There are multitudes of Evanses and Smiths among the Peers. *Who's Who* revealed the entirely appropriate choices: Matthew Evans of Faber and John Smith's widow.

The Turf was well represented by the Chief Executive of the Horse Race Betting Levy Board, the Chairman of the British Horse Racing Board, the Steward of the Jockey Club and Brough Scott. I saw no sign of Mr McCririck, who delivered a controversial address at Robin's Edinburgh funeral, nor was his name listed in the public prints.

The victim of that eulogy, the Prime Minister, was given a booby-trapped bit of Luke 16 to read – the story of Lazarus and Dives suggesting the torments ahead for those who suck up to the rich. He had to follow Cook's widow, Gaynor, who chose Micah and the injunction to 'beat swords into ploughshares and spears into pruning-hooks. Nation shall not lift up a sword against nation.' The anti-war message was finally rammed home by the choir with Byrd's beautiful setting of *Isaiah* 64:10: 'Your holy cities have become a wilderness – Zion has become a wilderness. Jerusalem is a desolation.'

The first eulogist was Madeleine K Albright. Their initial meeting was rocky but Colonel Gaddafi brought them together. Gordon Brown, manifestly at home in the pulpit, took as his text that quotation from Thucydides, engraved on a war memorial in Edinburgh, which I know as 'to famous men all the earth is a sepulchre'. He emphasised Cook's influence, 'woven into the stuff of our lives'; his failure to achieve his great, if misguided, ambition to reform the House of Lords; and, movingly, the admission that they were 'friends in the beginning and friends at the end; but, sadly, not enough in between.'

Peter Cook 'and friend' read extracts from his father's post-ministerial journalism – notably a passage about his two terriers. On George Bush he could draw a line under global warming; he could draw a line under Iraq; but when he saw Bush drop a terrier on its head, 'that was when he crossed the line!'

Chris Cook returned to his father's passion for the gee-gees, reading Larkin's lovely *At Grass*, his ode to retired racehorses: '...they/Have slipped their names, and stand at ease,/Or gallop for what must be joy,/And not a fieldglass sees them home,/Or curious stop-watch prophesies:/Only the groom, and the groom's boy,/With bridles in the evening come.'

Iris Villiers

1920-2005

St Paul's Church, Covent Garden

THIS SERVICE TOOK US warmly into the companionable world of concert artists, Lady Ratlings (the female equivalent to The Grand Order of Water Rats), 'the Skating Fraternity' and, gallant ushers, the Grand Order of Water Rats themselves, including the current King Rat.

Many Lady Ratlings had wonderful period names like Babs, Hetty, Val, Avril and Doreen. They referred to one another with splendid formality. We were welcomed by Laura Collins (Queen, Grand Order of Lady Ratlings) who gave variety artiste Ms Villiers her full title, 'Dame of the Order, Twice Past Queen, Iris', and so did everyone else, in rather the same way that on *Thought For The Day*, Muslims honour every mention of The Prophet, 'Peace be upon him'.

Past Queen Ann Emery, fresh from her triumph in *Billy Elliot*, was first up. She thanked Queen Laura who had known Dame Twice Past Queen, Iris for 23 years. Past Queen Ann then painted a picture of Dame Twice Past Queen, Iris' full career: her beautiful soprano; her lovely telephone manner; her wonderful south-coast home; her golden speaking voice; her husband, the late skating impresario Gerry Bourne; her parties; her Goodwood picnics, 'where the champagne flowed'; shopping at Harrods, 'caution thrown to the wind' in the Food Hall.

Her illustrious career came sharply into focus as we heard a tape of her singing *Some Day My Prince Will Come*. She also lent her voice to Ivor Novello's Maria Ziegler, touring for many months in *The Dancing Years on Ice*. Then, with Walt Disney's approval, she sang *Snow White On Ice* (Kenny Baker, who skated Dopey, went on to play R2D2 in *Star Wars*). Presented by Gerry Bourne and Gerald Palmer, she sang through editions of *Holiday On Ice* and recorded many albums. She was Dorothy in *The Wizard of Oz* and Wendy in *Peter Pan on Ice*. So popular did she become over the years that she was known as 'Mrs Wembley'.

Past Officer, Annette Sharville, representing 'the Skating Fraternity', celebrated Iris but pointed out the downside of her artistry: 'Being a double is not all fun when you are singing your heart out and your skating character is lying flat on her face on the ice.'

There were tributes from Roy Pike, with memories of walks along the Sussex coast, and Dr James Walsh. 'All artists give pleasure, some by arriving, some by leaving.' He also remembered 'helping a Lady Ratling from a trout stream' after one of the famous parties. Past Queen, Vice Chairman CAA, Pamela Cundell, vividly recalled a jealous prima donna's dismissal of our heroine when very young: 'That girl won't last! She's too short. No presence!' The music of Novello and Rodgers was devotedly interpreted by Ratling Linda Watts and Rory Campbell, accompanied by Water Rat Cliff Hall.

Dame, Twice Past Queen Ratling, Iris would have loved it.

Peace be upon her.

Ronnie Barker, OBE

1929-2005

Westminster Abbey

NEVER BEFORE HAVE I seen a eulogist 'milk' a pulpit. At first barely visible (big laugh), Ronnie Corbett then climbed on to a box, the better to be seen (bigger laugh). I doubt if he knew that Bishop William Walsham How, who wrote the first hymn *For All the Saints...* in the 1860s, was also less than five feet tall. Being too short for most pulpits, he travelled with a specially built platform wherever he preached.

The service had opened with the Abbey's great visual pun to celebrate Barker, the inspired word-player, and his most famous sketch. The choir, led by the Beadle and the Abbey clergy, was preceded by the Cross of Westminster – and four candles.

The great comic actor's career was deftly outlined. Richard Briers read the Prologue to Act IV from *Henry V* ('A little touch of Harry in the night'). Ronnie B had played truant to see Olivier's film and been spotted by his headmaster. Michael Grade contributed a paragraph from Barker's 'The Gentle Art of Corpsing' from his autobiography *It's Hello From Him*, which acknowledged his theatre career.

Peter Kay represented a younger generation of admiring comics. Having written a fan letter he was delighted to get a reply, apparently from HMP Slade, written by Ronnie as Fletch: 'I've managed to keep a clean sheet. That's only because I work in the prison laundry.' They continued to correspond. On one occasion Barker mused unfavourably on a 'biopic' of Peter Sellers. He speculated gloomily that one day he might be the subject of such a film. 'If you're offered the job, don't take it.'

We heard Ronnie's voice delivering his 'Sermon in Rhyming Slang'. The extravagances climaxed with a 'four-by-two-ish merchant' coming upon a 'small brown Richard the Third' in the street. Decency breaks through when the 'small brown Richard the Third' flies back to its nest.

After his pulpit 'business', Ronnie Corbett recalled the Glory Years in an address artfully tricked out in his monologue manner with sips of water, digressions and dropped pages. Playing Australia, Ronnie B and Harry Secombe tried to slim down. They reckoned that between them they shed the entire weight of Ronnie Corbett.

The long friendship, the family affection, the never-a-cross-word partnership were neatly and modestly summed up. 'Ronnie would write a sketch. I would queue for his lunch.' Then there was Ronnie B's retirement; their one-night-only reunion for a Royal Variety Show as 'The Two Fat Ladies'; the first signs of the last illness; and Ronnie B's amusement when he checked into a supposedly discreet clinic. The porter emphasised the secrecy again and again. Then he nudged Ronnie B: 'We 'ad that Danny La Rue in last week.'

'Forty years of unmitigated pleasure' were Ronnie C's words.

Worth celebrating.

157

Robert Carrier, OBE

1923-2006

St Paul's Church, Covent Garden

FOR ONCE IT WAS 'FOODIES' not 'thesps' who flooded to the Actors' Church. Welcoming them, the Rev Simon Grigg extended his invitation to 'entertainers'. Entertaining, in every sense of the word, was Carrier's great gift.

Auriol Evans interspersed the service with movements from Bach's *Cello Suite No 1*, an echo of the Bach which filled the cook's house in the South of France. We were also treated to five addresses and five readings from Carrier cookbooks, beginning with his claim that food is the only art that appeals to all the senses – no other tickles the nose and the palate.

First up was Sir Terence Conran, who appeared to move between tears and laughter in his account of a lubricated painter smearing mortadella over his face during a meal given in his honour in the famous eponymous Islington restaurant. He evoked that era which was both a Carrier and an Elizabeth David time; when Walter Boxer was pioneering the *Matelot* and the *Bicyclette* and when, I suppose, Sir Terence was stirring soups in his fledgling kitchen.

Talking of soups, Roy Ackerman read of Carrier's childhood. His grandmother's strong beef stocks were brewed at a farmhouse barn in the Hudson Valley and served with ham and lentils at the stroke of midnight on New Year's Eve.

Viscount Montgomery praised Carrier's work for the Restaurant Association, for changes in the licensing laws and for the showmanship he brought to his campaigns. A third reading limned in his arrival in dreary, wartime Plymouth, aged 21, en route to six revelatory years in Paris. And there was his delight in returning to England in 1953 to find London *en fête* for the Coronation and Sir Stephen Tallents, endlessly liberal with strawberries and cream.

Delia Smith worshipped Carrier when she was a washer-up. When she moved on to a women's magazine during the age of '10 exciting things to do with mince', he gave her confidence, encouragement and kindness. When she became a friend, she rejoiced in a prodigally floodlit Hintlesham Hall at the height of the miners' strike.

We had yet to hear of the five years in Paris when the phenomenal Naomi abandoned a marquis to cook for him, and from Alexander Barr, to whom he was 'almost a grandfather' during his Morocco period; or of his first sight of St Tropez and the rustic Provençal dishes, of fresh fennel and thyme.

Lady Carla Carlisle recalled the last few days. A week before he died, in a burst of energy, he booked to lunch once again at La Colombe d'Or and then had to cancel. She ascribed his philosophy, 'life is all possibilities', to his American legacy and to surviving the 'Battle of the Bulge'. She claimed among his inventions the celebrity chef, country-house restaurants, cookery cards; 'Even,' she said, 'he invented Robert Carrier.'